The Viewpoints of Stanley Marcus

A Ten-Year Perspective

The Viewpoints of

Stanley Marcus

A Ten-Year Perspective

University of North Texas Press   *Denton, Texas*

Requests for permission
to reproduce material from
this work should be sent to
Permissions
University of North Texas Press
Post Office Box 13856
Denton, Texas 76203–3856

The paper used in this book
meets the minimum requirements of the American National
Standard for Permanence of
Paper for Printed Library
materials, z39.48.1984. Binding
materials have been chosen for
durability.

Library of Congress
Cataloging-in-Publication Data
Marcus, Stanley, 1905–
The viewpoints of Stanley Marcus : a ten-
year perspective / Stanley Marcus.
    p.   cm.
A compilation of the weekly articles on
various subjects written by S. Marcus for
the Dallas morning news.
Includes index.
ISBN 0-929398-86-6
I. Title.
AC8.M355   1995   95-1451
081—dc20   CIP

Contents

Preface

A dozen years ago I was approached by a radio station to broadcast a daily 120-second commentary in which I could voice my opinion on any subject. It was explained to me that in lieu of any fixed compensation, I would give the local program to KRLD without charge, but that I would receive any income that might come from a national sponsorship.

This seemed to be an interesting, speculative way to become established in a medium in which I had no prior experience or following. The arrangement lasted for about three years, during which time I developed an appreciative audience, but no national sponsorship.

My experience as a merchant suggested to me that I had created a property that was an interesting avocation but had little likelihood of producing any income. I recognized that the only thing to do was to take the same approach I used as an active retailer, and that was to reduce the price of slow-selling merchandise until it found a buyer. If that procedure didn't move the goods, then give them away.

I finally gave the program away when I failed to find a buyer. But I had learned a lesson from the requirement of writing succinct messages that caught the listener's ear and held it through the brief period of the broadcast. I was forced to write economically, for every second counted. Shortly after the program folded, I received a call from Burl Osborne, editor of *The Dallas Morning News*, about writing a column for the paper. After being assured that I would be given the privilege of writing on any subject I might choose, without editorial censorship, I accepted with alacrity.

Osborne proposed that I write three columns a week, to which suggestion I demurred, on the grounds that three a week would be work, whereas one a week could be fun. He concurred with my decision, and at no time have my columns been altered or modified except for normal grammatical copy editing.

Ten years have gone by without missing a Tuesday deadline. I have never hesitated to express my opinion on a wide variety of subjects. Readers often stop me on the street to say, "I read your columns regularly, and there are times I don't agree with you," to which my reply has been, "I hope not. You should never concur with everything that any politician, commentator, or writer enunciates. If you agree with them part of the time and are stimulated to dissent part of the time, that's healthy and productive."

1984

Oh, For the Good Old Days

Many people bemoan the progression of time because things have changed; they're not like they used to be. They have a genuine nostalgia for the good old days. I don't; I spent my youth during the good old days, and I can tell you they weren't that good.

We complain today about litter on the highways, but in 1910 you had to watch your step and hold your nose as you crossed main thoroughfares. You had a phone, but it wasn't automatic. Trains ran, but they were dirty and hot in the summer and dirty and overheated in the winter. A train trip to New York took two nights and a day, and the train was usually late in arriving.

The summer was as hot then as it is now, but the only relief we had was the ceiling fan on the screened-in porch. You couldn't read at night in the summer, because the light attracted hordes of tiny insects which somehow penetrated the window screens and invaded your nostrils, ears, and hair.

Phonographs had to be hand-cranked, and after the first few playings, records became so badly scratched the production of the music was distorted. Cameras were "Brownies" and clumsy; the film was slow, and the results were invariably blurred and disappointing. Swimming pools were virtually nonexistent except for the one at the "Y," and it exhaled a chlorinated odor which still registers a pungent recall.

It would be misleading to depreciate everything of the past, for there were some things that were better than those of today. Take biscuits, for example. You rarely get a biscuit now that would compete with its counterpart of the first decade of the century.

3

We didn't have planes, and travel was excruciatingly slower, but the train food was infinitely superior to that served by most airlines today. You could also buy shoes which came in widths instead of being forced to accept one width for all.

Two things I miss most of all—letter writing and eccentrics. Modern telecommunications have all but destroyed the urge and need to write, and further development in the field undoubtedly will finish off the latter. Instead, we have computer printouts confirming a purchase, a reservation and a proposal of love.

There's no more chance today for an exchange of love letters between an Eloise and an Abelard than there is for a college football star to turn down a $5,000,000 draft contract. Where is there a father who is going to write meticulous letters of conduct to his boarding school son, as Lord Chesterfield did, when there are phone extensions in every room of the house?

Somehow, I don't think we have as many eccentrics in our society today as we used to have, and I miss them. I'm not referring to the Khadafys, the Khomenis, and the Hitlers, but to the harmless species that formerly were found in the courthouses, the domino parlors and other locations where the leisured were prone to gather. Maybe it is the fluoride in the water, the polluted air, or perhaps it is just a condition of standardization that has set in, encouraged by big business, big law firms and big business schools.

There are still a few left in this community [Dallas] who will remember with affection and amusement such characters as Tom Knight and his eccentric father, brothers, and sister; Jack Hyman; John Lancaster; Bill Kittrell; Bill McGraw; Pitchfork Smith and Louie Hexter. If you didn't know them I feel sorry for you, because you missed some rich experiences. These eccentrics were part iconoclasts, part free spirits, who didn't believe every news article because it had been put in print; they had no hesitancy in speaking their minds. They could be challenging, sardonic, humorous and crude.

They may well be becoming extinct or, at best, an endangered species. If you come across any, protect them and help them increase in numbers. Perhaps we can get the congress to set a day aside as "Eccentrics' Day" and even issue a 9 1/2-sided postage stamp in their honor.

Those Long-Haired Boys

In 1966, an incident in this city caused great waves of public indignation. Like so many things that tend to upset our equilibria and our stomachs, in retrospect it is difficult to understand why we reacted so violently.

I am referring to the period when males first started wearing their hair longer than was the accepted custom. There were a few murmurs when beards made their appearance; there were some caustic comments when sideburns began to lengthen; but when boys and men let their hair grow long, there was a social explosion. I should know, for I was caught in the middle of one of the most vicious barrages of epithets I ever experienced.

Here is how it all began. One day I read in *The Dallas Morning News* that a group of students who attended W. W. Samuell High School were suspended with threats of expulsion if they didn't recant, or at least recut. The defense of the students was that they had formed a high school rock and roll combo, and their contract with a booking agent stipulated they must maintain the length of their hair.

When I realized the social authorities were being serious, I felt the boys' civil rights were being violated, and I offered to finance their legal expenses to fight injustice. The case went through several courts, and the school officials were upheld in all instances. I didn't agree with the courts' rulings, but as a law-abiding citizen, I had to accept them.

My offer to pay their legal costs unleashed a tremendous storm of protest from all over the state, mainly originating, I later discovered, from two fundamentalist evangelical pulpits whose preachers urged their listeners to write Stanley Marcus and denounce him. Some of the writers blamed me for interfering in areas that were none of my business; others asserted that if the Lord had meant for boys to have long hair, he would have created them with long hair.

The fact our founding fathers wore their hair long seemed to have escaped their attention entirely. I replied to their letters of attack by reminding them every pictorial rendition I had ever seen of George Washington, Benjamin Franklin or Thomas Jefferson had shown them with long hair. I'm positive I no more convinced my adversaries than they did me.

The other day, I was stopped in the street by a nice looking young man who asked, "Aren't you Stanley Marcus?" I replied in the affirmative, and he said, "I'm one of those who was involved in the long-hair episode, and I never had the opportunity to thank you for your support." He is now a prosperous young businessman who still wears his hair on the longish side.

Today, the controversy has disappeared. Boys can wear theirs long, and girls can wear theirs short. No one seems to think there's a deep moral issue involved in the length of hair. However, a fight could arise tomorrow if some other element of the *status quo* were challenged. I'm confident that equally ridiculous ideas would be summoned to protect society and the nation from some equally unimportant change in our modes and manners. Would that we could become as charged-up about some important things upon which our future existence depends.

Myth of College Amateurism

Not only is business subject to antitrust laws, but so is academia, as the educational institutions found out when the Supreme Court ruled the National Collegiate Athletic Association was regulating the number of television appearances of college football teams in a manner bearing the earmarks of a "classic cartel."

The courts freed the schools from the restrictions of its own organization, so now college football and other sports will be regulated only by the marketplace.

The NCAA argument for its scheme was simplistic: "To give the smaller schools with weaker teams a chance to be telecast, we will apportion the appearances according to our best judgment." Similar cartel-like arrangements have been made time after time in many industries with equal logic, but all of them sooner or later have been tossed out because of anti-competitive aspects of the arrangement.

As a result, you may be sure you will see many more TV appearances of the big boys and fewer, if any, of the little fellows. It's the old story of "the rich get richer." Oklahoma, Texas, Georgia, Alabama, and the others that can muster the greatest talent will master the airwaves.

As they receive more revenues from TV, they'll have more money to devote to their teams. Colleges currently live under a myth that their teams are manned by amateur players, but every year, two or more schools are charged with offering illegal inducements to high school players to sign up.

Usually their agreements carry with them some extra inducements such as the use of a car, nominal jobs, clothes and other special privileges. Each year at least one college becomes extra aggressive in its solicitation efforts, and when caught receives a mild chastisement.

It has always seemed to me that colleges missed their big chance when professional football was just raising its helmeted head. They should have grabbed the franchises for themselves and fielded professional teams to represent them, using the earned revenues to support all the minor sports and an occasional educational course, possibly on Chaucer or Shakespeare.

They should have paid pro salaries without the fictional requirement of class attendance. If any players actually wanted to partake of education, they should have been granted that privilege at a nominal charge. That would have eliminated all the monkey business that goes on in most schools, relieving both players and administrators of the humiliation of semi-honest deals.

Texas has just gone through a dramatic bloodletting in coming to grips with the problems of public school education. One of the most daring challenges issued by the governor's committee, headed by Ross Perot, was the spotlighting of the question as to whether parents wanted superior education for their children badly enough to relegate football, drill teams and other extra-curricular activities to a minor role.

If that question was valid at the high school level, it is even more so at the college level. Let's face it—the field of knowledge has expanded vastly in the last two decades; it is difficult to cover the bare essentials of available subject matter in the normal four-year span.

Smart as we have been in opening new fields of knowledge, we haven't been smart enough to expand the twenty-four-hour day. Athletics as an essential part of the educational system should be given its due, but not a disproportionate share of the available time.

9

Business Lessons from the Olympiad

Now that the XXIII Olympiad has come and gone, American business may learn some good lessons from this super spectacular. It was organized by business leaders. It was publicized to the world by a free enterprise electronic press, all for profit.

There must have been a number of things that went wrong, but the total effect was so masterful the public was unaware of any minor blemishes. There can be a difference of opinion as to whether the games actually produced better international understanding or whether the label of amateurism isn't just a bit of wishful thinking. However, even the critics will have to concede it was produced efficiently and in the best of American Hollywood style, with the proper mixture of drama, color and schmaltz.

Whether the contestants were amateurs, semi-pros or government subsidized pros, they all were striving to achieve. This was the moment of personal accomplishment for which they had trained, dieted and disciplined themselves, foregoing the many temptations to compromise with the regimen that had been set forth as the road to victory. They entered the Olympic program with the single thought of winning. To that objective they dedicated their total efforts.

To win, they knew they would have to do their best every minute, every day of that arduous training period, every moment of actual competition. Half best wouldn't do. Even best, some days, wouldn't cut it; others would be doing better. This dedicated desire to be best was the magical quality the public perceived and applauded.

These atheletes from thirty-four different nations, speaking at least as many different languages, understood what they had to do to produce satisfaction. They knew they had to make the supreme effort to win whether they were in the lead or at the tail end; whether they were favorites or whether they were outclassed; they had to give it their best in every heat, every final contest.

This is the lesson American business needs to comprehend. Too frequently, we see new enterprises open with a lot of fanfare and promises, but a few months later, we discover the only thing they actually delivered was a facade of satisfaction.

They performed well on Mondays and Saturdays, but they goofed off during the rest of the week. All of us have had such experiences with new restaurants, automobile dealers and retail stores. Foolishly, many business leaders believe they can get by with a facsimile of quality rather than the genuine thing.

A colleague reports an experience he had in a neighboring city. He found it impossible to buy a mattress on Wednesdays in the branch of one of the nation's largest stores, because the salesman in the mattress department was off that day. The only way he could buy mothballs was by sniffing out their location. Another giant store in the same community had excellent stocks of hardware, but the salespeople had no comprehension that customers were capable and desirous of buying other articles in addition to the specific one they had come in for.

In a recently opened restaurant, the waiter, after cleaning the table, declared, "I guess you folks don't want any dessert," to which the guests replied, "Yes, you're right. We're going someplace else for ice cream cones."

No one has been able to establish a gauge to determine how much business walks out of any institution because of salesperson failure. The problem is not the sales staff; it is management which has failed to educate its staff, to supervise its staff and to establish and maintain standards and adequate compensation.

It's tough, but so is training for the Olympics. To win the gold on the track or in business demands the consistent performance of participants.

When and How to Complain

A common conversational topic is the decline of quality in merchandise and service. The blame is commonly passed on to inflation, but the causes are more deeply rooted.

Sales and service people usually receive the brunt of complaints, because they're closest to the incidence of dissatisfaction. Basically, though, management must take the rap, for if management is on the ball, sales and service people will be well educated in their jobs and responsibilities.

As businesses have grown in recent years, often to gargantuan size, managements' time and attention have been distracted from the two most important factors in any business—customers and goods—and turned instead to related organizational problems that are important but less vital to the health of the enterprise.

When the boss is not around or visible, workers may be less polite, willing or productive. Apropos this point, there is an old Spanish proverb, *El ojo del amo engorda el caballo,* or "The eye of the owner fattens the horse."

When business management devotes more time and attention to customers and products, two things happen. The customers come back, and the goods don't. It's so simple it is remarkable more business leaders don't go back to the fundamentals that made them successful in the first place.

Customers, too, have a responsibility to complain if they feel the quality of what they're buying doesn't come up to their standards. It is their obligation to complain, nicely but firmly, and to the proper individuals.

There is no use fussing at a saleswoman for a sweater that shrinks or a shirt that loses its buttons on the second washing. A waiter in a restaurant is not responsible for a tough steak or a hard melon, nor is the room clerk in a hotel to blame for soiled linen.

Management is the authority to which complaints should be addressed, for management can and will do something once it knows what's going on, and it is up to the customer to let management know.

Any company worth its salt welcomes complaints, for only by knowing its failures can management improve the product or services, which will result in greater satisfaction. Complaints need to be made politely, quietly and constructively.

This advice applies to a bad dish in a restaurant or to a defective product bought in a store; to the rudeness of a saleswoman, or to the disinterestedness of a hotel reception clerk. A customer should never feel embarrassed in making legitimate complaints.

There may be some difficulty in reaching the attention of top management, but one of the most successful devices for getting the attention of the chief executive officer is to send the letter of complaint in a box instead of an envelope. The theory is that secretaries have more respect for boxes than they do for envelopes and won't buck the box to a second assistant.

Beware Misleading Labels

The television screen shows the scared, freckled face of a little boy in trouble. "The distraught young woman at his side," the commentator says, "is Jane Doe, welfare mother."

The news media are constantly alert for quick, concise ways to categorize us. Even if I became a Buddhist monk and invented a cure for the common cold, I will always be identified in the newspapers as Stanley Marcus, retailer.

For better or worse, we are usually tagged with a label that shows how we spend the work day—John Smith, plumber; Mary Smith, lawyer; Jimmy Smith, student. If the title connotes a respectable, wage-earning status, or one condoned by current mores such as "homemaker," then there's no real harm done to the one so labeled.

But sooner or later the media must come to grips with the fact a title applied thoughtlessly may damage its recipient's reputation. Although men share this problem—as in the case of Al Capone, a former underworld character—the brunt of it is borne by women. A man is never identified as a welfare father.

If a person's means of livelihood is really an important part of the story, it should be important enough to warrant investigation to reveal all the relevant facts. John Smith, plumber, may cheat his customers by using inferior products. Mary Smith, lawyer, may specialize in finding legal loopholes for unethical conduct.

Jimmy Smith, student, may steal hubcaps or sell drugs to younger schoolmates. Jane Doe, on the other hand, may have accepted welfare as a temporary solution after she was laid off her steady, ten-year job when the plant closed, and she could not find another one in her town where unemployment of black females is twenty-two percent. Sue Doe, deserted housewife with three young children, may be stricken with a disease that does not permit her to leave her house.

There is a stigma to being publicly labeled a welfare recipient. The fact many of those on welfare have abused the privilege has cast an ugly shadow on those who are justifiably receiving legal, public relief.

Our society needs to reform the systems and supervision of welfare grants so the unworthy do not get on the rolls, but then it should allow those who do qualify for relief to be able to receive it without being demeaned. In our state of civilization, we should be smart enough to extend relief without depriving the recipient of dignified self-respect.

When innocent citizens are thrust into public view through accident or misfortune, the media could become more sensitive to the harm they might do through thoughtless labeling.

Taking Fashion Too Seriously

Fashion designer Bill Blass says those who take fashion seriously are "bloody bores."

This may seem like a peculiar statement emanating from a man who has literally made a fortune out of designing and selling women's and men's clothing, accessories and fragrances. In one respect, fashion should be taken seriously. The apparel industry is important to our economy, ranking sixth in volume, just ahead of building materials. It provides jobs and livelihoods for several million Americans. But with that caveat out of the way, Blass's concept needs closer scrutiny.

Anyone who has worked with the wonderful world of women's apparel has encountered fashion bores. They come in distinct categories—the consumer side and the supply side. Consumer fashion bores are those who allow some authority outside themselves to declare there is a right and wrong way to dress each season.

They diligently research the fashion magazines and trade papers to receive this divine wisdom and deck themselves out accordingly, whether it is head-to-toe ruffles or pinned-together punk. They agonize over every millimeter of hemline or cufflength, and consider any outing a failure wherein their outfits are not the prime subjects of admiring conversation.

There are those who enjoy the changes in fashion but who don't take them too seriously. They find gratification in beauty of fabric, design, and fine workmanship, and take pleasure in the fact that the garments they buy are different from the ones of a previous year. They don't talk about fashion—they just wear it. The fashion bore dresses to please others and ends up pleasing nobody.

But the consumer is not the only one who sometimes takes fashion with boring seriousness. The fashion press wastes millions of tons of paper on silly and banal reporting; the stores that preach the fashion gospel often are carried away by the gush of their fashion language and fail to report with objectivity and perspective. The fashion industry sells dreams and illusions to those who want to play the game.

However, there are many people who just want a warm suit to wear to work, a pretty print dress to wear to a party or an all-purpose coat to take on a trip to Chicago or London. They want it when they want it—not two months before or two weeks later. They have no patience with an industry that has such difficulty in regulating its production to meet the needs and demands of the majority of its customers. If any of those in the fashion business value these people less for their indifference toward fashion, then it is they who are the bloody bores.

1985

Orwell Ghost Still Out There

The year 1984 has come and gone and few of the prognostications made by savants after publication of George Orwell's book *1984* have come to pass. Or, if they have transpired, they have occurred so gradually we are barely aware of them.

A basic premise in the book is that a government that can restrict language can restrict thought as well. Orwell's imaginary totalitarian government wanted "Newspeak" to accomplish that goal; it sought to make the dreaded crime of thinking impossible, and by that restriction to better control the populace.

If you don't have a word for freedom, it reasoned, you are unlikely to have a group demanding it. So Newspeak became the only language in the world whose vocabulary got smaller every year instead of larger.

The first words to go were the cumbersome antonyms such as good and bad. Instead, things were either good or ungood. If something were better than good, Newspeak didn't allow it to be excellent or splendid; it was plus good, or double plus good and so on.

It is very easy to label some of the euphemisms currently coming out of Washington agencies as Newspeak, since they tend to encumber the language. This generation's wars have become "police actions"; murder in Central America is labeled "neutralization." Early in the Reagan administration, a tax increase was described by a Treasury spokesman as a "revenue enhancement." The Nixon administration had set the pattern by inventing "inoperable statement" for "lie," so the Reagan spokespeople thought nothing of describing the recession as "negative growth."

Such crippling of the English language can send a chill, no—a double plus cold—up the spine of an English major.

There have been the obvious abuses of freedom by the totalitarian rules, but that is to be expected of them. That is their means of self-sustainment.

We in the free world need to fight them vigorously on every front as evidence of violations of human rights occur, but we need simultaneously to resist efforts within our own democratic governments to curtail freedom of speech and expression, to resist the establishment of areas of departmental secrecy on subjects that probably have been already publicized in the *Congressional Journal* or *Discovery* or *Science.*

There is always the chance a hostile government can profit by the freedom existent in a free society. The only way to protect absolutely against leakage of information is to eliminate freedom absolutely. This extreme is equivalent to killing the goose that lays the golden eggs in an effort to protect the price of gold. Obviously, this in no way suggests traitors who sell or give away our national secrets should be dealt with in any other way than as traitors.

Newspeak or government gobbledygook cannot be proliferated without the acquiescence of the news media. It is time for reporters to remember their First Amendment rights and call things what they are and not what someone else thinks they should be.

We have passed 1984, but it could still happen here.

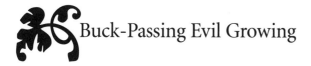 Buck-Passing Evil Growing

When Harry S. Truman was president, he had a sign on his desk which became famous. It said, "The buck stops here." It was a reminder that, as president, his was the ultimate responsibility.

It has been taken for granted through the ages that the leader takes responsibility for his followers, his business, his organization. That is both the privilege and the burden of leadership. For better or worse, the person in charge accepts the praise or the blame. But the last handful of presidents has not always accepted that tradition.

It seems the change started with Vietnam. President Nixon never tired of reminding us that the tragic war was all the fault of the escalation by President Johnson. President Kennedy told us he was merely trying to clean up the mess created by the policies of President Eisenhower. President Johnson didn't hesitate to point out it was President Kennedy who first sent over military advisers.

More recently, once it became obvious our economic problems would not be solved through a painless tax cut and a magically balanced budget, we have been treated to the unpleasant spectacle of blame-laying all the way back to the Roosevelt administration. President Reagan has blamed Congress, the Russians, the Nicaraguans, his economic advisers and almost anyone within reach to whom he could pass the buck. Apparently, Nancy is the only one who does not share the blame, for it has been said love is myopic.

It is partly our own fault that our leaders have resorted to this immature finger-pointing at their predecessors. We elect them because they promise easy answers to complex questions, solutions simple enough to be hammered home in a one-minute television spot. Once in office, rather than admit to the complex nature of our economic realities, they again resort to the simple, by simply saying, "Hey! It's not my fault. It was that other guy!"

One of the first lessons taught to ten-year-olds is "to stand up and take your medicine if you're wrong. Don't pass the blame on to someone else. If it's your fault, admit it and take the punishment."

It seems to me they used to cite a fellow called George Washington for the way he handled the cherry tree situation. It is up to us to stop the buck passing. When others say, "It's not my fault," we must write them that we didn't elect them to be apologists, historians, judges or philosophers, but to be problem solvers.

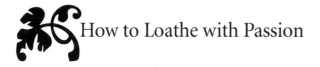# How to Loathe with Passion

The yeast of life our present time seems to be lacking is a sense of style. I ran across a twenty-year-old clipping that reminded me that, if done with style, even loathing can be delightful.

The great columnist, John Crosby, in one of his essays from London a few years back, wrote of the complaints of Diana Menuhin, wife of concert violinist Yehudi Menuhin. "Innumerable people hate modern times grouchily, but Diana hates them with a smile," he said. "One of my favorite pastimes is to listen to her denounce the twentieth century. She does it with such high, good spirits."

On this particular day, Diana was upset at the disappearance of tradition. "Convention is bad, but tradition is good," she said. "If you eat strawberries in November, you kill all the sense of waiting for the proper season. It's like installment buying. You get the chair too easily. If you have to do without movies for six months, or without sweets for a year, the chair means something."

She continued: "The same thing with flying. Travel doesn't mean anything unless it takes a little time." That's why she loved American trains, she said. "I passionately adore them. I used to like getting on the train in New York for San Francisco and just going to bed for two days and three nights and reading six books cover to cover. I don't like French trains. They go too fast. They get you there. American trains *never* get there."

She didn't like marrying young, either. "A man now gets married at eighteen, and he can expect to live to be eighty, so he's expected to be monogamous for sixty-two years. Can't be done. In the old days a man got married at twenty-five and died at fifty. He had to be faithful only twenty-five years, which is more reasonable."

If there are any two words that best describe this part of the twentieth century, they must be "instant gratification." We don't want to wait for anything, we want it now. What's more, we get it now, thanks to special payment plans, plus indulgent parents, and the opportunities for employment on part-time schedules. Any qualified person can trade five evenings a week, or put in a sixth day working in a shopping center to make the payments on a new car or possibly to buy a new coat.

We are still marrying young, buying on credit and coping with impossibly slow American trains. What we're missing is the wit of people like Crosby and Mrs. Menuhin to teach us to loathe our times with style.

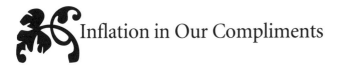# Inflation in Our Compliments

We're all familiar with the term "inflation" when we're using it to talk about how much or how little our dollar will buy, but there's another kind of inflation to which we can't pay adequate attention.

Money is not the only thing that is inflated during our lifetimes. We have inflated our way of giving praise and compliments. We do it in both word and gesture. For example, we frequently hear something described as "terrific" when it's merely OK; or "fabulous" when it is just good. "What do you think of your new car?" you ask a friend, and he says, "It's fabulous." So what is he to say confronted with something truly fabulous, like the Grand Canyon?

We are inclined to blame word inflation on advertising. It has long since made us insensitive toward superlatives such as "Super!" "Giant!" and "Once in a lifetime!"

But in recent years, there has been a trend that gives evidence to the fact we might have done it on our own. The culprit is the standing ovation. Years ago, an outstanding performance at the theater or the concert hall brought the audience to its feet with cheers and applause.

Such an ovation was as rare as it was spontaneous and, as such, was a fitting response to show honor to performers who had made an extraordinary effort. But nowadays, it seems that if the orchestra manages to start and finish a piece together or the actors don't muff their lines, then half the audience jumps to its feet with "Bravos!"

Maybe I have been so lucky lately that I have managed to see only outstanding performances, but common sense and my own critical facilities make me doubt it.

Unsophisticated audiences are likely to react to artistic performances in one of two ways. One is to sit on their hands and not applaud because they don't know what is good or bad. The other is to over-respond by reacting to a symphony in the same manner as a football crowd does to a forty-yard pass. Both reactions reflect a lack of knowledge which is not necessarily the fault of the members of the audience.

Perhaps the programs or the conductor should indicate by printed word or by gesture, "Here is the place to applaud." Just because the conductor appears to be in a frenzy is no reason for the audience to follow suit. Undeserved standing ovations seem wrong to me on two counts. Not only do they leave us with no adequate response to a truly great performance, but they must surely offend the performers when they know they have merely done their job.

The Controversies of Art

Old Town in Albuquerque, New Mexico, is a cottonwood-shaded plaza by the Rio Grande, surrounded by adobe shops and churches. It was also not long ago the focus of a heated controversy, one that is chronic to our democratic way of life.

Albuquerque's picturesque Old Town offered the perfect site for a public sculpture of some importance. Luis Jimenez is a Hispanic painter and sculptor who has received increasing recognition in the art world for his fiberglass reinterpretations of Old West myths. He seemed to be the logical choice for the job. All the good citizens of Albuquerque were in agreement on these two points. They haven't agreed since. Jimenez decided on his theme—a Romeo and Juliet kind of legend about a tragic pair of Aztec lovers. Jimenez tried to capture this poignant story with the figure of a grieving man holding the body of a beautiful maiden. But the people of Albuquerque didn't see star-crossed lovers. Indians and Hispanics alike were offended by what they believed to be the depiction of the violence of the Conquistadores toward the native population.

The details differ, but the controversy surrounding public art is an old story. This particular case was in Albuquerque, but not too long ago it was Dallas debating the pros and cons of the Henry Moore abstract that now graces City Hall or in Washington, D.C., where a federal agency was under attack for having located a sculpture by Richard Serra in front of a government office building. In Paris there has been a public outcry over the glass pyramid designed by famed architect I. M. Pei to serve as a new entrance to the Louvre.

29

Ever since Michelangelo's "David" was installed in Florence, public art has sparked hours of public debate, frequently acrimonious and always passionate. Naturally we are concerned about the appearance of our cities, but the concern goes deeper than cosmetics.

Public areas belong to all of us, and all of us have a right to hold an opinion on how they are used. That does not mean public art should be determined by plebiscite, or that if we dislike the chosen piece we should attack it with more than words. There is no method that is foolproof, but the best results have occurred when art has been selected by art-knowledgeable individuals such as Lorenzo the Great in Florence or by competent communities comprised of qualified art authorities.

If we left the selection of art to a public vote, we would get sculpture and painting of the quality of some of our elected officials, who make good first impressions but don't hold up over the long run. Art speaks not only to our aesthetic senses but to the hidden symbols we all live by. It is encouraging that, in an age where our senses are saturated with junk food, music and prime-time TV, this dialogue still takes place.

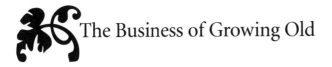 The Business of Growing Old

Growing older is something that happens to all of us, but feeling old is, more often than not, something we do to ourselves or that we allow others to inflict on us.

When I was a youngster, I had the privilege of knowing a wonderful gentleman many years my senior. Well into his eighties, he had an energy and a zest for life enviable at any age. I asked him how he did it.

"Do what?" he scornfully retorted. "I'm going about my business, like you should do!" But after he had properly reprimanded me, he relented and explained. "You see," he said, "nothing really changes just because you're older. You are *exactly* the same person. You don't feel any different—you're just older."

Now that I am approaching eighty myself, I have begun to appreciate my mentor's insight. Life's experiences may smooth over a few of our rough edges, but I am essentially still me. I am as eager as I ever was to learn scuba diving, to wear the latest styles, to enter law school, to bicycle across Europe, to learn to operate a computer. But if I do not do these things, it is because I think—or I am afraid others will think—I am too old. This fear has nothing to do with ability or even with chronological age. My head still turns at the sight of a pretty young woman; I continue to appreciate a trim pair of legs, a well-shaped bosom.

A musician I know, already accomplished in her field, expressed her desire to study for an advanced degree in a specialized area of music. "That's a great idea!" I said. "When do you start?"

"I don't," she replied. "I'm too old." She is twenty-nine!

Where is it written that the joy of learning belongs to the first decades of life? The truth is, the more years we accumulate, the more urgently we should be encouraged to seek out new physical and mental challenges. The stimulation of the learning process is more rejuvenating than any mythical fountain of youth. The process of learning new things, of conquering fresh problems, is the elixir that keeps one young. That was advice I learned from my ninety-seven-year-old mother before she died.

I would like to think age brings wisdom, but I am not so sure that's so. It does bring a greater appreciation for the good things in life, since we know firsthand they're fleeting. I guess that is wisdom enough at any age.

Let's Hear It for Some Couth

Not too long ago, the average person consulted an etiquette book only when planning a wedding. Now, largely thanks to Judith Martin's popular Miss Manners column in *The Washington Post* and her recent book, manners are coming back. Throughout the social upheaval of the last couple of decades, there has remained a small underground where invitations and gifts were always promptly acknowledged, introductions were made without stammering, and multiple silverware taken in stride.

Good manners make all our interactions with one another much more pleasant and agreeable. If such greasing of the wheels of the daily grind is becoming more widespread, so much the better, but it is doubtful if the pundits who are hailing the returning interest in etiquette as the potential cure for everything from illiteracy to nuclear warfare are correct.

In the seventies, there was some downright rudeness going on. It probably served to highlight some important questions about our society. It was good for us to ask whether opening doors for women was a sexist ploy. We had to re-examine our notions of correct entertaining—based on a stay-at-home wife with a household staff—to the reality of the working woman with little help and less time. But now that those questions have been asked, and we hope answered, we can get back to those time-honored little niceties that make life more pleasant for us all. According to an article in *Time* magazine, good manners are "in" again.

Marjabelle Stewart, founder of etiquette training classes for children in 700 department stores, has become the nation's crusader for couth. She says, "We are emerging from a rude, rebellious period. Everyone is tired of slobs." In the last fifteen years, Ms. Stewart's classes have instructed more than 160,000 children from Tuscaloosa to Chicago in how *not* to become slobs. They've learned how to handle utensils and sip soup and other tasteful habits. They've conquered the complexities of room service, restaurants, concierges, elevators, and front desks—just in case, I suppose, they ever run away to a fine European hotel. In a class designed for pre-teen girls, aspiring young women learn how to curtsy and how to dine in a formal atmosphere by candlelight. A young boys' class instructs in the fine art of dining in a men's club, though I suspect a class in how to dine in a school cafeteria might be more useful.

Children aren't the only ones benefiting from Ms. Stewart's lessons in *savoir faire*. She also works with companies to teach the social graces to backward business executives, particularly those so busy climbing the corporate ladder they don't know how to act when they arrive at the top.

On the subject of manners, George Bernard Shaw's Henry Higgins had it right when he told Eliza Doolittle, "The great secret is not having bad manners or good manners . . . but having the same manner for all human souls."

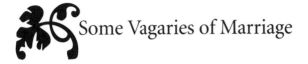# Some Vagaries of Marriage

Those living in the West have difficulty in believing there are parts of the world, even the civilized world, where parentally arranged marriages are still in practice. We are so accustomed to the concept that youth marries for love that it seems impossible that young people in India are willing to accept the marital partner choices of a father and mother.

Recently in Varanasi (formerly Benares), an old friend, a maker of sari fabric, introduced me to his handsome thirty-year-old son. When I asked if he was married, I was advised the parents were in the process of searching for a bride for him. I was shown the newspaper advertisement which specified a fair-skinned, slim, young woman with an educational background similar to that of the son. The ad concluded by saying, "Girl only consideration."

It was obvious from my facial expression that I didn't understand that line, so my Indian friend explained. "That means that the only thing of importance is the girl herself, not the dowry." I asked if most Indians were of the same mind. "No," he replied, "only in the upper classes would that be true. The vast majority insist on a dowry, which may consist of money, livestock, a motorcycle, and/or a TV. Do you want to see the answers we have received to date?" he asked, and without waiting for a reply, he began opening letters from the morning mail. I glanced over a half dozen of them, all neatly typed with curriculum vitae just as we would encounter in reading applications for a secretarial position.

He tore out an advertisement from the morning paper which was sponsored by the directorate of social welfare in Delhi. It read,

"Another sacrifice at the altar of dowry." The text went on, "Unable to bear the torture at the hands of her in-laws, Meena sacrificed her life at the altar of dowry. So many daughters-in-law in the society have died like this. Your own daughter or sister will be a daughter-in-law one day. Let us take a vow that we will neither give nor accept dowry. It is a crime to accept dowry. Keep yourself away from this social evil."

"What effect will ads like this have?" I inquired. "None for the time being; perhaps the custom will disappear in fifty years," was his answer. I persisted in my inquiry, "Does the youth still put up with parental selection? As a Westerner, it is inconceivable that young people in this day and time would still be willing to have mates chosen for them."

My friend turned to me and said, "My parents selected for me, and it worked out well. My father's parents selected for him, and it worked out well for him. I know so much more about such matters than my son; my father knew so much more than I."

Then with a twinkle in his eye, he asked, "What is your divorce rate in the United States?"

"Oh, about sixty percent, I believe," was my answer.

"Well, here it is two percent. Which method works better?"

Learning Is Its Own Reward

The period of the Italian Renaissance has always been attractive to us, in large part because it was a time when men and women defined themselves by their own criteria, not by that of some outside authority.

The Renaissance is sometimes defined as the rebirth of learning. It brought about the flowering of architecture, painting, sculpture, writing and scientific discovery. It left us a legacy of beautiful buildings and unforgettable literature and art. It was a time when people studied for the joy of it, and great discoveries in the sciences were made as a result. Nowadays, we tend to think that research and scholarships are the provenance of the universities and the giant laboratories of space-age technology.

Not so, according to a story in the *Los Angeles Times.* There is a growing underground of amateur scholars. These new Renaissance men and women are doing serious work in astronomy, art, literature, even computer science. Not affiliated with a university or aided by a governmental grant, they pursue their passion while supporting themselves with full-time jobs in non-related fields. We all know that John LeCarré's fictional superspy, George Smiley, is a respected authority on medieval German poetry. A loner, Smiley enjoys his solitary pursuit of Goethe and his peers.

But the more gregarious independent scholars in the past would seek outside recognition for their work. Ironically, the recognition of this phenomenon comes about as the result of the research of an independent scholar, one Ronald Gross, who, with a government grant, has identified and learned the needs of other independent scholars.

It's always exciting to discover that a business associate has a quiet, legitimate second life, unpublicized, but quite real. It may be the hankering of a Houston octogenarian who invents things to improve the conveniences of life; or it may be the analyses of the growth cycles of orchids that command the free time of a Dallas lawyer; or it may be the study of Southwest Indian pottery that made Francis Harlow, an atomic physicist at Los Almos, one of the world's greatest authority on prehistoric pots.

There has always existed more to learn in the world than man has time to achieve, but today's expanding frontier of knowledge is so vast that we need several lifetimes even to penetrate the world of knowledge at hand.

It is all right to seek academic degrees and public acclaim for independent study, but there are dedicated scholars who have discovered that the joy of learning can be an adequate reward in itself. It seems too bad, with so much to be learned about our world, that so many of us haven't undertaken serious continuing education.

Waste Done Best by Military

When we read reports about waste in government at all levels, it is quite natural to berate the agencies, departments and individuals responsible. The frequent incidence of these exposures is probably responsible, in part, for the growth of private enterprise in areas formerly considered government monopolies, such as prison operation, mail and package delivery and garbage collecting. Extravagant payments for commonplace articles offend all thoughtful citizens.

Only occasionally, though, do we become aware of overstocked inventories of supplies. As any retailer knows, the hardest problem in operating a store is to keep inventories in balance, which means at proper ratio to sales volume. To accomplish this objective, the merchant must push out his older, aged stocks to make room for the new. It often takes reductions in price, job-outs, and other techniques to get the stocks cleared. Once that is accomplished, the process starts all over again.

No other method will give the customer the assurance of finding the particular size and color of a garment she wants, or guarantee that a man will find the kind of new hammer recently put on the market. There is no other way to have everything, other than maintaining a huge stock of out-of-style merchandise that nobody wants.

It is a curious fact that the military doesn't like, and in some instances, doesn't maintain, inventory control. Consequently the services don't know what they have until they run out of a given item.

It is doubtful if the civilian supplies in government and state agencies and departments are managed with as much sophistication as Dillards's cosmetic stock. The ideal person to manage government supply departments would be a graduate of a department store or even a country store on the square, for they both recognize the hazards of dead stock.

Only on occasion are we treated to a revelation of the contents of a government warehouse. Not often enough, to be sure, for it represents our tax money tied up in antiquated goods and products.

However, in England last month the prime minister, Mrs. Margaret Thatcher, took the bit in her jaws and named a new Whitehall waste catcher, after learning a few unpleasant facts about the out-of-date, out-of-use, out-of-style products in some of the government's storerooms. For example, they found a 120-year supply of cardboard map holders, enough ballpoint pens in one department to last fifteen years, and enough filing bags in the energy department to last 1,000 years. Another department was reported to have on hand a twenty-five-year supply of carbon paper, even though photocopying machines have virtually eliminated the use of carbon copies. They discovered a set of offices stacked from floor to ceiling with metal typewriter tables, and to everyone's surprise, a million tins of VIM (a cleaning agent).

The British are looking for annual savings of $400 million (approximately a half billion dollars) without any contributions from the military. The one area the waste catcher will not cover is defense, "where spending is widely seen as the most extravagant of all," according to an article in the *London Standard*. In this respect, America and Britain are not far apart.

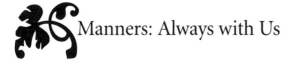 Manners: Always with Us

Manners have been a subject for discussion, writing and argument ever since the cave man left his cave. Society has always considered the way people behave in public a matter of general concern and subject to criticism and even conformity to the accepted mores of the period.

From the sixteenth century onward, there has been an abundance of books written to advise the uninformed, particularly children, on what to do and not do. They probably were the original "how-to" books, one of the most popular categories in bookstores today. In the nineteenth century, the British public was obsessed by good manners, and books on the subject were printed in normal size and in miniature for boys and girls to study at odd moments. Good conduct standards were rigid and not subject to individual interpretation or prerogatives. Private schools were the repositories for the rules and regulations necessary to turn out young men and women who knew the social graces.

It is not unnatural that the subject of manners is of continuing interest in a mobile society, for there is a constant stream of people moving from one echelon of the social order to another. We used to frown on this idea, saying, "We are a classless society." That simply isn't true, and never was true in America. What we probably were trying to say was, "We have classes in our society, admission to which is open to those whose achievements in the professions and commerce have been noteworthy enough to place them among the existing leaders of our community."

The qualification, doubtlessly, assumes that in having achieved eminence, the individuals also have amassed an adequate amount of the currency of the realm to enable them to pay their way. This is a simplified explanation of "society" in every part of the nation. No one in this country was born with divine rights, despite the fact some believe that to be true. How else do you explain the rise to social eminence of such names as Rockefeller, Carnegie, Mellon, Phipps, or Vanderbilt?

The Hockaday School in Dallas, under the rigid supervision of its founder, Miss Ella Hockaday, placed the value of tasteful conduct for her young female students on at least an equal scale with the conjugation of Latin verbs and the memorization of logarithm tables.

In the middle part of this century, during World War II, a youth-inspired social explosion occurred which broke most of the precepts of our society. Convention was flouted, mainly because it was convenient. Restaurants that had required jackets and ties for its male guests surrendered to the insurrection and compromised that only shoes would be *de rigeur*. Blue jeans were worn to weddings, gloves and hats were tossed into the ash can, college students brought their boyfriends and girlfriends home with them to share communal quarters, all in the name of the new revolution.

Most resort hotels suggest that dry bathing suits in public areas are acceptable, but "please don't bring wet suits and sand into the lobbies." However, there are still some bastions of tradition that have changed only *one iota*.

Recently during the New York hotel strike I took refuge at the Harvard Club, where I was duly impressed by the club's adherence to the past, much more so than the university itself. I came across this notice in the bedroom:

> Members and guests shall be properly attired at all times, in accordance with the regulations of the House Committe. Dungarees, shorts and tennis shoes are not considered appropriate dress within the club.

Joggers please use the hallway leading by the coatroom to exit and enter the club. It is respectfully requested that you exit in a hasty manner.

The House Committee

The final sentence was the Harvard Club's capitulation to changing times.

Media Slow to Investigate Sports

It seems strange that journalists who have revealed so many cases of skullduggery, dishonesty and governmental corruption through painstaking and courageous investigative reporting have failed to blow the whistle on collegiate recruiting. With so many fine reporters on Texas papers, it would seem they could have exposed the violation of NCAA rules by many of the Southwest Conference schools long before now. Granted that suspicions are not legal evidence, it seems that determined effort over the past twenty years would have yielded some results.

Average fans, with no inside knowledge, had more or less suspected that hanky-panky was going on, so when the final revelations began to appear this fall, only the university presidents and deans expressed surprise.

It may be unfair to cast stones at the sports writers without throwing a few at sports editors and managing editors as well. After all, it is the latter who had the final responsibility to authorize and fund an investigation of public housing discrimination, of financing fraudulently valued condominiums, and of the overcrowding of penal facilities. Venturesome reporting in the area of public interest is the material on which Pulitzer Prizes are won.

This subject was not nearly as dangerous as writing about a narcotics scam, or infiltrating a strike headquarters or even the locker room of the Cowboys after their loss to the Bears. Sports writers had to be aware of the boosters that every college possesses—or, more accurately—that possess every college. They must have heard the rumors of athletes on alumni payrolls, or jocks riding around in expensive cars, or gut courses for football players.

44

Of course, substantiating those rumors with documentation may be another matter, and I am not suggesting that the newspapers report rumors. The press may be frustrated, in fact, by its inability to document these scams which operate on a cash-only basis and are clouded in secrecy.

It is doubtful that there was a conspiracy of silence, for too many were involved. Perhaps the press was selfish; it didn't want to destroy the exciting stories emanating from winning local teams. Perhaps they felt that the sports public was aware of the story and didn't give a hoot.

Wrestling enthusiasts understand that the sport isn't to be taken seriously, but is to be regarded merely as an exciting exhibition. Perhaps writers reasoned that the public doesn't want to know something bad about its athletic heroes, and regards the bearer of bad news with the historical punishment accorded to such purveyors of unpleasant information.

The *Daily Oklahoman* ran a disclosure a few years ago on the illegal sale of football tickets by players. This exposé caused no public indignation, but did result in threats to the life of the reporter, which caused him to move to another city for self-protection.

Whatever the reasons, the press that gives us such good coverage in a wide area of sports events came to bat with the bases loaded and struck out!

1986

Our Differing Kinds of Grief

Cultural differences between the Orient and the West are often self-evident, but no incidents are more demonstrative of these differences than the corporate reaction to the death tolls in airline disasters. The extreme contrasts of behavior are not cited as criticisms of airline officials or public figures in our country, but they do raise a lot of questions.

After the fatal collision in August of the Japan Air Lines Boeing plane against the side of a mountain, resulting in 520 deaths, it was reported by *The New York Times* correspondent: "The president of Japan Air Lines faced the relatives of victims of the world's worst single-plane disaster and bowed low and long. He turned to a wall covered with wooden tablets bearing the victims' names. He bowed again. Then, in a voice that sometimes quavered, Yasumoto Takagi asked for forgiveness and accepted responsibility."

This burial service marked the final memorial sponsored by the airline. For Takagi and his employees, this marked the culmination of a two-month exercise in public accountability. Early on, Takagi had promised to resign as an indication of the responsibility of his position. In November, Takagi undertook a cross-country pilgrimage paying visits to victims' relatives to make a last apology before retiring in December to atone for the crash.

Perhaps the Japanese are not accustomed to airplane tragedies; perhaps their cultural heritage dictates a different response from that of an American or European airline president. I don't recall any airline official or chief executive officer of a chemical corporation in our country offering to make such personal sacrifice.

Perhaps the legal terms are essentially different in the matter of public liability. JAL paid $1.5 million for the memorial services and is sharing with Boeing an estimated $100 million compensation fund.

I am afraid that in the West, bad news comes so frequently we tend to shove it off the front page as quickly as possible. We have deep regrets, but we show little real grief. Everybody is so busy passing the buck from the airlines—to the control towers, to the Federal Aviation Agency, to deregulation, to inadequate maintenance—that there is little time to express deep sorrow.

Only recently, when President and Mrs. Reagan went to Fort Campbell, Kentucky, to extend their personal sympathy to the families of the troops who were killed in the chartered aircraft, did one get a sense of actual grief in this country. Compassion comes from action and not statements to the press.

 What Happened to Biscuits?

Nowhere is the beat of the distant drummer to which I march more compelling than in the matter of food. Just when the world is going crazy over croissants, I began wondering, "Whatever became of biscuits?" When I was growing up, biscuits, hot and steaming from the oven, were the everyday fare of the mid-day and evening meals. Hot rolls, or yeast buns as we called them then, were expected for Sunday dinner. Packaged bread was called "light bread" and was served only by indifferent young brides when they were sure their mothers-in-law would never find out about it.

I understand that the children of today relish and even prefer this insipid product. Back then, we kids rolled it into pea-sized balls that bounced across the table. But biscuits were a staple, a standard by which the rest of the meal was judged, yes, even timed. If the answer to, "How long 'till dinner?" was, "I'm just putting the biscuits in," we knew exactly when our meal would be served. Although a cook was known by the quality of her biscuits, she was allowed the choice of two schools of thought. There was the moist and flaky school where the texture of the golden crust varied little from the creamy matter inside. Then there was the crispy crust school where the crunchy outside was achieved by dipping the dough top and bottom in bacon grease before baking. But either type had to have tall, straight sides, with tops and bottoms an even plane exactly perpendicular to the sides.

This engineering feat was achieved by deftly blending the ingredients with just the right amount of strokes, judicious kneading of the dough, and the lightest possible touch of the rolling pin, a skill acquired through years of practice. Biscuits were served hot and were immediately split open and spread with fresh butter. If seconds were required, the cook timed things accordingly and had another batch ready to come from the oven at the appropriate time. Biscuits were never reheated in my childhood world. Instead, those that were allowed to grow cold went with us in school lunches with a bit of sausage inside for a sandwich.

The demise of everyday biscuits came about the same time commercial biscuit mixes were invented, a fact I find to be significant. Oh, I know you'll find something masquerading as a biscuit in some of the restaurants today, especially those that specialize in chicken-fried steak or use buckets and styrofoam as serving vessels. But they're just not the same. Their bland, salty taste is to the real biscuit what a corn chip is to a garden-fresh ear. With a little luck and good timing, you can still find fresh corn.

I'm afraid the real biscuits have passed into nostalgia along with the Light Crust Dough Boys and "Please pass the biscuits, Pappy."

TV Stereotypes Businessmen

All the way from the little house on the prairie to the Big Apple, today's television may be doing for the image of businessmen what Bonnie and Clyde did for banking.

From *Dallas's* oily villain, J. R. Ewing, on down, most businessmen on television are depicted as crooks with Mafia connections, cheats, employers of professional arsonists, and worse still, jerks, clowns and buffoons. With few exceptions, nowhere on prime time is there anyone remotely resembling such admirable businessmen of the past as Joseph C. Wilson of Xerox, Edwin Land of Polaroid, Alfred P. Sloan of General Motors, or Thomas Watson of IBM.

A *Time* magazine report observed that the Media Institute studied 200 prime time shows in all three major networks. It revealed that two of three businessmen are shown as foolish, greedy or criminal, and that almost half of all work activities performed by businessmen involved illegal acts. Owners or managers of big business were almost always filthy rich, with gigantic houses, servants and limousines. There was some honor among small businessmen, but most of them came off as ineffectual fops. Even in those rare instances where TV's businessmen looked good, it was on a purely personal level. Rarely did it involve the socially or economically productive behavior that is demonstrated daily by thousands of business executives.

Are nice guys boring, or is art imitating life? Personally, I think neither is the case. Some of the most exciting dramas are being enacted in the corporate boardrooms as management's struggle for survival against takeover bids from rival companies, or in the marketing department offices as new products are researched and tested to meet intensive domestic and foreign competition. In the vast majority of these cases, there are honest difference in values, not evil maneuvers to steal something away from a rightful owner.

Television writers seem to have a universal disregard or lack of understanding of the values of organization, authority and profit. At times they would appear to be antagonists of the free enterprise system. All business leaders aren't the supermen that their public relations departments depict them to be; all are not crooks as the *Wall Street Journal* reports on crime might suggest; all are not connivers. The vast majority are just out to make an honest buck.

 The Lost Art of Salesmanship

Americans used to be known as the world's best salesmen. Recently, it has become difficult in most stores to encounter that quality of salesmanship, if indeed you can even find a salesperson.

A few years back, I made up my mind I would not buy anything I did not urgently need unless a salesperson was convincingly persuasive. As a result of this self-imposed discipline, I have saved $46,734.

Want to know a few things I didn't buy? An automobile, for one. I called a dealer I knew and inquired whether his new models had arrived. "Yes," he said. "How are they?" I asked. "Fine," he replied. I said, "Thank you." He made no suggestion of having a salesperson drive me around the block or of lending me one to drive on the weekend. He never called back, nor did I receive a phone call from one of his salesmen. So, I didn't buy a car.

I visited a luggage shop in search of some lightweight luggage. A salesman started to show me some pieces, when he was summoned to the telephone. He came back and was just embarking on the merits of his product when the phone rang again. I waved goodbye to him. He knew me, but he never called to apologize for his poor service. That night when the manager asked what sort of day he had, he probably replied, "There weren't many buyers today, only lookers." I don't blame him, but I do fault his management, which had not emphasized that the customer at hand takes precedence over the one on the telephone.

The advertisements of the new thin watches impressed me, but since I had a perfectly good twenty-five-year-old watch, I was looking for some compelling reason to junk it and buy a new one. When I asked a jewelry salesman why I should buy it, he looked around and finally said, "It's newer." That, I knew, but it was not sufficient reason to make a purchase.

The volume of lost business to retailers and industry as a whole is appalling. Some merchandise can be sold without benefit of a salesperson, but many products require an introduction and presentation. If stores are dedicated to self-service, then it is incumbent on them to organize displays and stock for easy shopping, but if they profess to supply service and charge for it, then they must provide adequate, well-versed sales assistants. Otherwise, they should resort to vending machines which can be more efficient and a lot less costly than humans who don't know their stock or why a product is worth buying.

Stores and sales staffs have been spoiled by years of easy selling. During the Depression, I learned that the best way to sell anything was to encourage the prospective customer to feel the article while I discussed the benefits he would receive from it. We treated every prospect as though we wouldn't see another all day. And some days, we didn't.

What Young Execs Don't Learn

Thousands of aspiring executives will be graduating from the business schools in which the management of money has been the central thrust of their education. *The New York Times* reports starting salaries in the neighborhood of $45,000 for MBAs. Here are a few fundamentals they haven't been taught.

An ability to design is essential to an architect, but in addition he must learn structure, form and materials. In business, money management alone is not enough to assure a successful career. From my observation, most of the young executives are disappointed to find that the business they've joined does not require immediate financial reorganization. Their perspective is such that they don't want to get behind a sales counter to learn about customers or behind a machine to learn about products.

Many have not even learned the rules of politeness, such as standing up when a visitor comes to the office or walking the guest to the door when he leaves. I am sure the schools have not taught that a letter of inquiry is due a *prompt* answer; a letter of complaint an *immediate* one.

I doubt if the business schools offer advice in telephone etiquette, with the suggestion that telephone calls not be taken while there is a guest in the office, and that all telephone messages be answered the date of receipt, and that secretaries should never state, "The boss is in a meeting." That information is offensive to the caller. It is much easier for her to say, "Mr. So-and-So is away from his desk. May I ask him to return your call?"

Not only young executives, but some old ones as well, are remiss in expressing thanks for a gift, a news clipping, a luncheon, or even a bit of information. A "thank you" may not be remembered, but a failure to say thanks can be stored in a memory for a decade.

Most of the young executives are so eager to be exposed to all phases of business that they don't stay in one job long enough to develop expertise. Sometimes, job jump-arounds are the fault of management which switches people around to fill new positions caused by rapid expansion. The results are the same. Too many young executives know something about many things, but not a lot about anything. In their race to the presidency, many young executives lose sight of the fact that some jobs within a company take years to master.

The fact that young executives are in great demand and are offered large starting salaries does not add to their own humility or to their list of earned assets.

How To Avoid Rip-off Art Fakes

Many people are hesitant to purchase a work of art for fear they may be ripped off by an unscrupulous dealer selling a fake or a reconstructed object.

There are, of course, deceptions in every line of business, art included. The best protection I have found is to deal with a reputable art merchant who has a proven track record for knowledge and fair dealing. View both the itinerant dealers and the ones offering bargains with a degree of skepticism, for bargains in art rarely exist.

The best one can expect today is fair value with a guarantee to exchange for something else within a reasonable period. More mistakes in buying art have been made attempting to beat the market, for good works have an international value of which every dealer from here to Cairo is aware.

An established art dealer is just as proud of his reputation as is a good jeweler or doctor. If he makes an error in judging the age or condition of a piece, he will refund your money without question. He has the experience to guide him and access to laboratories with devices that can establish such matters as age, over-painting, restoration and condition.

I have made a few mistakes in my career as a collector, and in each case it has occurred when I violated one of the rules I have just suggested. When I went to Egypt some years ago, I was eager to buy an antique limestone slab engraved with figures and hieroglyphics. A friend had given me a letter to the keeper of antiquities in Luxor, who, he thought, might help me with my quest.

The official told me that in his position he could not find a piece for me, but would be happy to pass judgment on anything I located. I did find one I liked very much and asked him to look it over. The next day, the keeper called and said, "Mr. Marcus, you have very fine taste. I've examined the piece and it is beautiful. The only trouble is that it is a reproduction. However," he said, "it was made 500 years ago!" I had not realized that copying had been going on that long.

The best a collector or buyer can expect to get these days is fair value. Gone are the times when great bargains could be found in faraway lands or from uninformed shopkeepers in our country. Today, valuable information is so easily available there are very few ignorant sellers. Almost every dealer has a copy of the latest Sotheby's or Christie's auction catalogue in his desk drawer.

Miracle of Spring Gardening

During the spring and early summer, I revel in the miracle of the flowering of the trees and the blossoming of the tulips, peonies and forsythia. I am not much of a gardener, but I have come to have particular appreciation for those who had the foresight to plant flowering trees.

There is an old Chinese proverb that says, "If you want to be happy for a few hours, get drunk. If you want to be happy for a weekend, get married. If you want to be happy for a month, kill your pig and eat it, but if you want to be happy for the rest of your life, take up gardening."

I don't know who the sage was who made such a convincing case for the joys of gardening, but it is one of my regrets that I did not learn the pleasure of being an active gardener until just recently. For years, I had been content to be a pruner, and while I get a lot of satisfaction out of pruning bushes and trees, clearing away the underbrush, and tidying up the flowerbeds, that is secondary to the joy of seeing something you planted come into bloom. My wife has introduced me to the pleasure of planting seeds and seedlings and learning to watch them mature into flowering plants. It's like magic, and I must say it is both gratifying and humbling to realize we can assist nature to bring such beauty into the world.

Obviously, gardening is good for you. It exercises muscles that only calisthenics can equal. It gets you into the outdoors, into the sun or the shade. In addition to all else, gardening is an optimistic endeavor, for the act of planting carries with it your expectation that your efforts will bear flowers, barring unfriendly insects, floods or drought. This state of optimism is not a bad thing to cultivate by any means.

Some streets in our city bear evidence to the fact that ten, twenty or thirty years ago there were residents living here who had the vision to plant flowering crab apples, redbuds, and other fruit trees. They set an example, and the neighbors responded.

Other streets stand in stark contrast, for obviously no one set a standard of inspiration, and as a result they have no spring color. What a shame! It is never too late to make amends by planting a single color-bearing tree. One usually gets you ten.

When spring comes and I see the flowering redbud trees, I am impelled to show appreciation to nature by planting another tree. Just think what we could do for our neighborhoods and our cities if each of us planted one flowering tree a year.

The Sad Decline in Quality

Do you think nothing is as good as it used to be? Well, you're right; there has been a decline in quality. Very little we buy is as good as it was prewar. The automobiles, suits, shirts, shoes and dresses we buy are not as good as they were.

The reason for this decline in quality is related to the delayed effects of the industrial revolution, starting in the late eighteenth century with the invention of the steam engine, which replaced hand labor with steam power. This eventually led to mass production and subsequently to mass distribution.

It helped produce greater quantities of goods at lower prices and made goods plentiful. Finally, the difference in costs between machine and hand production virtually forced the latter out of the market. The machine can make some excellent things, but when it is pushed to maximum production speed, it is likely to turn out some pretty shoddy merchandise.

During World War II, we had what is generally called a seller's market, a situation in which there is a greater demand for goods and services than there is a supply. "Take it or leave it" became an unspoken motto. That in itself was enough to encourage a decline in quality.

With the added element of inflation to production, quality really began to slide. The two greatest enemies to quality are bigness and public ownership. As businesses have become larger, it has become more difficult for management to maintain a personal supervision, and in most instances, quality suffers.

To remedy this condition, it is up to management to improve

the education of its supervisors in the basic philosophy of service that made businesses successful in the first place. When goods were artisan-made and distributed, the public benefitted from the pride of the producers. As soon as the artisan took in a partner or sold shares, he was forced to compromise, for he had to provide dividends to his investors.

This is not a condemnation of public ownership, for it helped democratize capitalism, but nonetheless the management of the public-held company may be less sensitive to public reaction and demand than individual ownership.

The buying public has become accustomed to shoddy quality and service and no longer complains as vociferously as it once did. Unfortunately, producers and sellers interpret silence as a lack of interest in quality.

Learn to complain, politely but firmly, when you receive what you believe to be inferior goods or services. Don't register your complaint with the salesperson or the waiter, but with the owner. He will listen.

Managers and Public Service

As businesses have become larger, with multiple branches and plants, the quality of goods and services for the most part has declined.

Proprietor ownership in many companies has been replaced by professional management, consisting of men and women who have been educated in the management of money rather than the preservation and perpetuation of fine quality. There may be examples of professional managers who actually established businesses dedicated to fine quality, but if there are, they are rareties. Essentially, professional managers are caretakers and accumulators capable of running established companies and improving operating profits.

Nowhere is quality more closely related to owner management than in the restaurant business. In March a few years back, I was dining at a New York restaurant and ordered melon for dessert. I remember the month, for it occurred to me that anyone ordering melon in March had no right to complain if it wasn't good. The owner, attired in his chef's hat and apron, walked through the dining room, speaking to the guests he knew and smiling at those he didn't.

My melon arrived, and although nice in appearance, it was hard. I was barely able to dig out a spoonful. When the waiter came back to clear the table, I made no complaint, for after all it was March. In a few minutes, the waiter returned with another slice of melon and said, "The chef thinks this might please you better."

The owner-chef, seeing the melon minus one spoonful, immediately knew something was wrong; and on his own volition, without a complaint from me, replaced it. That is a quality peculiar to proprietorship. In today's stores, it is difficult for the customer to identify management, much less ownership. Time was when floor-walkers were dignified men dressed in striped trousers and cutaway coats with white carnations in their lapel buttonholes. That attire designated them as management representatives. They were omnipresent, and if the customer had a complaint or a query, it was easy to find these men and get assistance. They have been replaced by department managers who carry no baton of authority, and who are barely identifiable or visible, so busy are they with other responsibilities involving paperwork instead of customer attention.

In Chicago recently, I observed that Carson, Pirie & Scott had decorated their floor managers with large red carnations and apparently eliminated their paperwork responsibility, allowing them to concentrate on the needs of the customers.

# Novel Way to Select Our Pols

Over the years, I have been privileged to know a number of men and women who have run for and held public office. They are a breed apart, and that's what worries me.

A friend who ran unsuccessfully for Congress recently told me, "The emotional and financial costs to a candidate are so great you have to be crazy to run for office." I am not sure all our congresspeople are crazy, but certainly they are politically ambitious and financially favored, or they wouldn't have survived the campaign rigors necessary to achieve these competitive posts.

They are representatives, the closest link you and I have to the federal government. But are they representative of us? Perhaps, but only by the coincidence of geography. Where in Congress can we find the professional musician? The podiatrist?

I would like to propose that we select our representatives by lot, just as we do jurors. If we are satisfied that we provide justice in this manner, why not apply it to public office? The names of all citizens eligible to vote would go to the pool—the old and young, rich and poor. There would be no excuse, other than serious illness or disability, for failure to serve a single two-year term.

Just think of the advantages. A congressperson chosen by chance would have no obligations or political debts to repay. All the monies now given to political action committees could be saved or donated to worthy philanthropies. Overnight, we would get rid of the most dangerous cancer in our system of democratic government—the bought and paid-for officeholder who is currently beholden, whether he be president or senator, to those who financed his campaign.

Such a randomly selected group would be so diverse and unpredictable that it would throw the lobbies into chaos, eliminating special interest pressure, and since any one of us might find ourselves in Washington the next time around, voter apathy would disappear.

Just as former French Premier Georges Clemenceau observed, "War is much too serious a matter to be entrusted to generals," so we are beginning to realize that government is too important to be left to the politicians.

Learning to Judge Quality

My definition for quality in a product is something that performs what it was designed to do regularly and consistently, and with a pleasing aesthetic form. The article might be costly, such as a Barguzin sable coat, or inexpensive, like a Bic cigarette lighter.

All it takes to learn about the quality of almost anything is a little application and a lot of curiosity. The acquisition of this knowledge need not cost a cent. You can learn about automobiles, pearls, Oriental rugs, paintings, rare books and textiles by using the same technique. It is known as comparative shopping.

To learn about diamonds, you should visit four or five jewelry stores successively. Ask to see a one-carat diamond. Tell the salesperson you don't know anything about stones, but that you might be buying one in the future. He will point out the differences in color and the flaws that can be detected only under magnification. He will acquaint you with the difference in shapes, as well as the variety of cutting techniques.

Go to another store while this newly gained information is fresh in your mind and repeat the performance. By the time you have reached the fourth store, you will be surprised at what you've learned. Plan the visits early in the morning or late in the afternoon so as not to interfere with customers who are there to make purchases. In a month, repeat the same procedures, but inquire about diamonds a size larger or smaller.

All of this won't qualify you to become a professional diamond merchant, but you will be able to make a personal purchase with a great deal more assurance. This method will prove useful to you in any field. Using it, you can develop a working knowledge about the colors of pearls, the techniques of artists, the qualities of furs or the characteristics of different kinds of Oriental rugs.

You will find that most sellers are only too glad to impart their knowledge to a willing listener. Through the process of comparing quality grades or periods of production, your eye will gradually learn to discriminate and discern the differences. Be careful, though. Nowhere is it truer than in industry that a little knowledge is a dangerous thing. Don't ever try to outsmart an expert seller just because you know a little something. He knows much more.

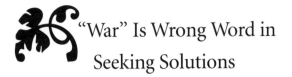

"War" Is Wrong Word in
Seeking Solutions

Every time we turn around, somebody is declaring war, and always for a good cause—war on poverty, war on crime, war on drugs. Yet when the shooting is over, the problems remain.

Why is it that whenever we want to get rid of some pressing social problem we declare war on it? Those are strong words to use when talking about alleviating human problems such as poverty, alcoholism or urban blight. It is our nature to want to make an all-out assault and get rid of whatever it is that's plaguing us once and for all.

To use the word war is an indication of the way we want to deal with problems; total mobilization to get the job done. But war also brings with it the connotation of guns, marching armies, killing and being killed.

If the human race has learned any lesson at all, surely it has learned that war brings not solutions, but devastation and bitterness. Most important of all, we have learned that one war sows the seeds of the next. If we examine more closely this facile use of words, we might see that a war on problems, like a war on nations, has its victims.

Perhaps the use of the word "war" makes it easier for us to go out and rough up some individuals while we leave the root cause alone. Our war on urban blight succeeded in dislocating some poor people from their homes, while inner-city slums remain. Our recurring war on drugs usually winds up putting a few addicts in jail, while the major suppliers continue to live in luxury; and the misery that causes some to turn to drugs remains unexamined.

This observation is not meant to diminish the severity of the problems. To the contrary, our society needs to take action on a wide variety of social ills and find ways to cure them, permanently and peacefully. Unfortunately, most of them require years of study, perseverance and experimentation to develop meaningful solutions.

"War" suggests "blitzkrieg," a quick and powerful thrust that overcomes all opposition.

In recent months, there have been newspaper headlines: "Federal reserve declares war on S&Ls," "Congressman declares war on starvation," "President declares war on leaks." Currently, the word war is used exclusively in rhetoric, while in the field of arms it has been replaced by "skirmish," "attacks," and "maneuvers." The politicians and the press must have their slogans, and war is certainly an attention-getter. But, any use of the word "war" suggests creation of more problems than it solves.

School on Wheels a Fine Idea

I have always thought that if I ruled the world I would make sure every child in America spent at least one summer on the road to observe for himself the magnificent variety our country offers. My own choice would be a lengthy tour of the scenic wonders and the prehistoric cultures in the deserts and mountains of Arizona and New Mexico. But anywhere would be OK as long as it was reached by ground transportation so the child could experience for himself the vast distances that make up the space between sea and shining sea.

We keep hearing about what a mobile society we are, and anybody who has tried to travel during a holiday weekend will attest to the fact. But I've been encountering a great many young adults lately who haven't ventured 100 miles from where they were born, not even for vacations.

These are the same youngsters who exhibit a kind of passivity and lack of curiosity that baffles those of us who find the days all too short and the hours all too few. A taste of travel might not cause them to develop a zest for life, but it could at least give them a sense of perspective.

That is why I was so pleased to hear about the Traveling School, a program developed by the public school system of Santa Cruz, California. Students spend a semester traveling on a yellow school bus with a teacher and three aides. So far, they have been through Florida, Louisiana, Texas, Colorado, Oregon and British Columbia, studying not only the terrain but attitudes and customs of the people they meet. Students range from seventh to twelfth grades and must abide by strict behavioral and academic standards. They are required to keep journals and to write frequent papers while on the road.

Now in its fourth semester, the program is considered to be a great success, with eighty percent of the students showing improvement in their regular classroom performance back home again. The program costs taxpayers nothing. Parents, local benefactors and fund-raising projects pay all the expenses.

Those involved in the project agree it requires extraordinary dedication on the part of teachers, parents and the students themselves, but that the results are worth it. That's good news, indeed. The bad news is that the Traveling School is a last-ditch effort to rehabilitate truants, drug addicts and dropouts.

It's not that I am against such rehabilitation, far from it. But it's my dream to give *every* kid such a chance to experience firsthand the purple mountains' majesties, even if he has had the misfortune to make straight A's and be respectful to his elders.

And who knows? If we put all our kids on the road regularly, maybe the stimulation to their imaginations would keep them from turning to the stimulation of drugs in the first place. Let's face it, in our overprotected society there is not much room for adventure for the good kid. Look at how we celebrated the Fourth of July this year. We tell our kids it's wrong for them to go out and pop firecrackers on their own, but OK to sit there like a lump and watch somebody else pop them for us on television.

Fireworks on television! Naturally, any kid with spunk will reject this concept. "C'mon, get real," they tell us.

Miles and miles across America on a school bus—now that's real.

Obfuscation and Pomposity

Obfuscation is a four-syllable word to describe the process of darkening or obscuring. It works well with relatively simple words or statements. It is most frequently employed in public relations releases and in explanations made by "official" spokespersons in government and industry alike.

Its purpose is to make something simple and intelligible into something ponderous and difficult to understand. It comes about as a result of the writer's or speaker's desire to confuse and bewilder the reader or listener.

Oftentimes, it is a device for padding the job description of a position in either a corporation or public institution. Obscuring the basic facts enables a jobholder to enhance the importance of the job, or at least the sound of it, and to inflate the status of the position.

As a result, we see the creation of pompous corporate titles, such as "office of the president." This is supposed to conceal the fact that the president of the company can't make up his own mind, so he establishes a four-headed team that issues statements or policies that insulate him from the heat.

In the increasing desire to differentiate between the thick layers of vice presidents (assistant VPs, VPs, senior VPs and executive VPs), the corporate world yearns for such titles of distinction as "royal VP," "super VP," "supreme VP," but these don't work.

Consequently, the art of obfuscation tackles the titles of jobs, on the theory that they are inflatable to the point of disguising the real functions. "Personnel director" becomes transformed to "director of human resources," and "operating manager" is renamed "director of strategic analyses," and a "display manager" is designated "director of visual display." An accountant becomes "manager, productivity and asset performance," and a maintenance manager is called a "director, facilities management."

Who's kidding whom? Certainly not employees, who don't regard themselves as "human resources"; certainly not fellow executives, who look with amusement as an incumbent officer indulges in this bit of buffoonery and puffmanship.

Physicians used to prescribe calomel to purge their patients. Industry and public institutions need a similar cathartic to rid themselves of this verbal garbage and to get back to calling things what they are in words clean and comprehensible.

Humor: An Essential Business Skill

In the pantheon of young business executives, there are gods of success, diligence, alertness, punctuality, timing and memo writing. But alas, there is none for humor, which I view with dismay.

According to Richard J. Cronic, who heads an executive search firm in Rosemont, Illinois, eighty chief executive officers were called and asked: "Have you found that younger executives with MBA degrees have a greater or lesser sense of humor than others?" The vast majority of those responding checked "lesser."

Why? Heightened seriousness among young people in general since the 1960s seems to be one reason for this attitude. But at least part of the blame lies with business schools. While most of the 170 business school deans who were polled acknowledged that there was probably a correlation between humor and executive success, they generally agreed that their institutions were turning out men and women who were more tough-minded.

Although the MBAs generally see themselves as the best and the brightest, the most energetic and ambitious, a growing number of corporate managers look on them as arrogant amateurs, trained only in figures and lacking experience in both the manufacture of goods and the handling of people.

In this century, there has been a tendency to approach all problems, business and political, with dead seriousness; we attempt to solve them by a partial attack conducted with vehemence and vengeance; rarely do we try to dissolve them with satire and humor.

All of this is particularly obvious in business profile interviews, political speeches and newspaper editorials. Aside from Art Buchwald, Gary Trudeau, and Russell Baker, there are few writers who even think to use the skills of satire to decimate the opposition as Dean Jonathan Swift did with such success.

Young executives who show no humor are missing an important attribute. Success in any field depends on influencing others, and wit is still one of the best tools around for doing that.

Said Ralph Benedict, Jr., the owner of a lamp company in Philadelphia, "How true it is. Humor is a lost commodity in today's world. Guess we shall have to wait for the Japanese to export it."

1987

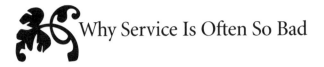# Why Service Is Often So Bad

Time magazine, which usually is on top of the news, has belatedly discovered that customer service in the United States has gone to pot. Its researchers from different areas of the country have awakened to the fact that most department and mass distribution stores are practicing self-service, that these same stores concentrate more of their training efforts on how to operate the electronic cash register than on the more trying task of supplying customers with needed information. It cites a customer who chided a supermarket employee for "failing to say thank you," only to get the answer, "It's printed on your receipt."

Time tells of the experiences of a customer in New York who waited four weeks for delivery of a bed because the store lost its paper work, and of another one in California in which a deluxe refrigerator was broken by the workman installing it, necessitating several visits by other workmen to repair it. The magazine concludes that, "The simple reason service workers have so little attention to give is that business often overworks them to save labor costs and keep prices low."

The usually alert *Time* has missed the basic causes of the decline in service, although it is eminently correct—albeit delayed—in its recognition of the situation.

In 1979, I wrote a book called *Quest for the Best*, which dealt with the decline in quality of both goods and services. In it, I concluded that wartime shortages forced many stores to accelerate the already existent trend toward self-service; after the war, rising minimum wages and other increased costs of doing business made it difficult to return to previous standards of staffing.

In the book, which proved to be a bestseller, I suggested that postwar prosperity and the shortage of goods created a sellers' market that influenced salespeople and those rendering service to become rude and imperious in dealing with the public. Unfortunately, the consumer business never recovered from these unhappy wartime influences. As companies became larger, their managers became burdened with other responsibilities and paid less attention either to their customers or to the quality of the merchandise they sold.

In my judgment, bigness is one of the basic causes of the decline in the quality of goods and services. A second cause is public ownership. A publicly owned company suffers from the lack of personal incentive to satisfy customers; a privately owned business, managed by the owner, will normally outshine the publicly owned one. By necessity, a publicly owned business is profit motivated, with satisfaction of secondary consideration; a privately owned one is customer-driven, realizing that profits are the result of having rendered satisfaction.

It is unlikely that the large publicly-held companies are going to pay enough attention to service and quality until they begin to feel it in their income statements; that's the only thing they understand.

Customers who frequently feel outraged by poor quality fail to remember that in a free society they hold the final power—that of patronage. If they don't like the way they are being treated in a store, a bank, a gas station or an airline, they should write letters to the president in protest. If this procedure hasn't produced results in the past, try sending the letter in a box. As previously pointed out, secretaries may buck a complaint letter to the sixth vice president, but they are most likely to see that the box is placed on the boss's desk.

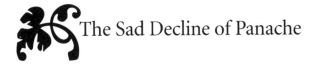# The Sad Decline of Panache

Panache is a French word which translates into "plume of feathers," but its meaning has to do with how the plume was used. In *The Three Musketeers*, the leading characters wore hats with plumes of feathers, which they doffed with a dashing flourish. Thus, the word became associated with flair, self-confidence and courtliness.

This is a quality that is becoming less and less evident in modern life as we become more and more concerned with efficiency of production and cost control. Panache is one of the first casualties caused by an economy-concerned executive. "We can do without the flourishes," we can almost hear the cost cutter exclaim.

Oftentimes we become so obsessed with cost control that we tend to cut the frills simply because they are obvious and not because they represent substantial savings. By the same token, we frequently leave major cost items undisturbed because they occupy the status of sacred cows.

In cost-cutting meetings, I have heard executives say, "Well, no one can argue about eliminating this or that. It will save us $100 a month." My answer has not been standard, for in many cases I've replied, "Yes, I can argue with that proposal. It will save us $1,200 a year, but it will depreciate the way we appear to important customers. It will standardize us and make us look commonplace."

Standardization is one of the major trends in our culture and society. It may be cost efficient, but if it discourages consumption of domestic goods by forcing those who want distinction to buy foreign merchandise, the so-called savings go out the window.

Here are a few cost-saving examples I have run across in recent weeks.

Case one: I was breakfasting in a coffee shop, in the center of which was the toast section manned by a bright-looking young man wearing a tee shirt. The shirt was slightly soiled, with an appearance suggesting it had been worn in a soccer game. The owner of the coffee shop saved money by requiring the toast maker to provide his own attire. How much more professional he would have looked had he been dressed in a clean white chef's jacket and a *toque blanche* perched on his head. The panache of such a costume would have increased the customers' confidence that the toast-and-egg-maker was a professional and not a jack-of-all trades. It would also have suggested that the cooking process was conducted under maximum sanitary conditions, and that the eggs were as fresh as the chef's attire.

Case two: A friend paid $150 for a costume jewelry necklace for his wife's birthday and was shocked when it was delivered in a brown corregated box stuffed with wadded-up newsprint. He was indignant and returned it for credit. He purchased another necklace elsewhere. So who saved money by destroying the panache of the package?

Case three: A new partner of a restaurant decided to economize by replacing the traditional vase of fresh flowers with a bouquet of artificial blossoms. There is nothing wrong with artificial flowers, except that they imply that some of the food ingredients on the menu may also have been replaced by ersatz products. No flowers, or even a vase filled with crinkled colored paper, would have been better cost savers.

Panache is a rare quality. A few people have it; most do not. It cannot be taught, but it can be encouraged. Flair doesn't make the world turn, but it makes it a lot more pleasant.

There are very few businesses or cultural organizations that don't profit by flair. It thrives on recognition and compliments. It is well to take the time to applaud it. Otherwise, panache may be headed for extinction.

Guide to Being a Good Customer

In my fifty years in the retail business, I have waited on every type of customer, from the shy shopper who turns shopping into charades, to the "I-hate-to-shop" shopper who foredooms the whole process. There are both good and bad shoppers, just as there are good and bad retailers and salespeople.

I feel particularly sorry for the small retailer, who is more likely to be taken advantage of than the employees of a large store. A bad check is bad for any business, but it is particularly hard on the "mama and papa" type of store that has no staff to make a collection follow-up. The late return of an expensive piece of merchandise may be a drop in the bucket for a large store, but it may be the difference between a profit and a loss for a small one.

There is an art to being a good salesperson, and there is an art to being a good customer. "Good" customers unquestionably earn better service than "bad" ones. Over the years, I've developed six simple rules that make any person a better customer.

The first rule is: Never be a pushover. Don't buy from people who don't make an effort to sell to you. Unless you are really convinced by the seller, walk out with your money still in hand. There is always an eager, enthusiastic salesperson who wants and deserves your business.

Two: When you return to make a purchase you had been "sold" on previously, ask for the person who originally showed you the item. Some salespeople work on a commission, and all are judged by how much they sell, so make sure the person who "sells" you gets the credit.

Three: Don't say you are just looking if you aren't just looking. Too many people consider it a stock response to a salesperson's queries. These same people often leave a store frustrated with the lack of assistance.

Four: Report bad salespeople to management, and report really good ones, too. Both the bad and the good benefit by constructive critiques.

Five: Try not to harass your salesperson about store policies. Even if the store requires a driver's license, birth certificate and three credit cards to cash your check, try to hold your tongue. The salesperson did not make the rule. It is better to find out the manager's or owner's name and give him or her a piece of your mind.

The sixth rule supersedes all the others. It is simply this. Temper the first five rules with the pleasant realization that you, the customer, are always right. You hold the upper hand—you can always shop elsewhere.

Simple Acts of Courtesy Disappearing

It doesn't require much more energy to be thoughtful than it does to be thoughtless. Yet somehow it seems that fewer and fewer of us are able to manage simple consideration these days.

There was a time, well within memory, when certain elementary rules of courtesy were expected—helping others, for example, and respecting one's elders.

Just a generation or so ago, virtually no citizen over the age of sixty would ever have been obliged to stand on a crowded bus. Today, the public conveyances are full of elderly standees, while teenagers sit staring blankly ahead.

We have, quite simply, become a society where it is entirely legitimate to give a damn only about oneself.

Invariably, we are responsive to the needs of others in times of emergencies, like fires or earthquakes, yet we fail to give consideration to social problems such as homelessness and acquired immune deficiency syndrome until we see them as personal threats. What is more worrisome is not that a lot of old people have to stand on the bus, or even that volunteer programs across the country are lacking in personnel.

What is a concern is that this selfishness threatens to undermine the tradition of generosity which has always characterized us as a people. We continue to be very generous with money while becoming parsimonious with our personal commitment.

What is curious about all of this is that there is a good deal more warmth in the air now than ever before. Every time we dial information, the operator tells us to "have a good day!" The advertisements say, "Have a Coke and a smile!" and "Reach out and touch someone!"

It is almost as if ad copy has crystallized our expressions of human need and rendered us less capable of responding to others at all. Incessantly bombarded by platitudes, we simply do not listen as well anymore—or see as clearly. Or, finally, feel as deeply.

People who show consideration to others in person are often apt to be very inconsiderate when using the telephone. The technology that permitted the development of the "call waiting" device has to be regarded as one of the more retrogressive developments of the century. This telephone signal is anti-democratic, anti-humanistic and inconsiderate.

The best way to deal with it is simply to hang up when someone says, "Wait a minute, there's another call coming in." That injunction is like a slap in the face, for what is inferred is, "Someone more important is calling me. You wait."

So each of us is left with our conscience and the choice of whether to "reach out and touch someone" or continue to look out for Number One. The right choice can do a tremendous amount of good, setting even cynical strangers to speculating on the possibilities of the human heart.

 The Corporate Dollhouse

If you're working for a large company, in any position from a file clerk to middle management, and you think your job is driving you crazy, you may be right.

Ever since Henrik Ibsen, the great Norwegian playwright, created the character Nora for his play *The Dollhouse,* novelists and dramatists have been exploring the tragedy resulting when mature and competent people are forced to behave in immature and incompetent ways.

Women, of course, have been obvious victims, but some recent studies indicate that our highly structured, rule-bound style of management, which has evolved as the result of the growing bigness of business, creates environments that are just as bad for mental health as was Nora's dollhouse.

As business and government have grown bigger, management style has shifted from individual initiative toward the establishment of rules and standard operating procedures to cover every contingency. When everything is done "by the book," individual decision-making disappears. Then, forced into rigid patterns, competent adults wind up adapting to behavior patterns that, considered in other contexts, are symptoms of mental illness.

This startling conclusion was reached by a research team that administered standard personality tests to MBA graduate students and found results consistent with those of people who suffer from depression, paranoia, hysteria and compulsive behavior. The test subjects were more interested in adhering to procedure than they were in relating to their fellow human beings.

One definition of creativity is the ability to know when and how to break the rules. An employee who never makes mistakes by simply avoiding innovation never accomplishes much either.

It is highly unlikely that either business or government is going to grow smaller, so the quest for our social system is to learn how to deal with bigness and how to avoid being overcome by it. That is one of the most important challenges facing our society today.

This problem is one deserving the close attention and study not only by the universities but by companies like General Motors, Citibank, Xerox, IBM and planners in the federal government.

Bigness has provided some great benefits to society; it has also been responsible for some of our greatest problems, yet unsolved. Corporate bigness, unchecked and unimproved, actually may force changes in our theory and method of government.

# Enemy of Creative Thinking

We have heard since childhood that we should develop good habits and break bad ones. But it may be that any habit is bad because it relieves us of the necessity of thinking.

I know a man who has a job that requires creative thinking, but who has a tiny office. In a space no longer or wider than a tall man, he crowds a desk, swivel chair, bookcases, two file cabinets and a fifty-gallon aquarium. Every time I see him, everything in the tiny room is completely rearranged. In over a year, I have yet to see him duplicate a pattern.

For a long time, I said nothing about his restless office, assuming that moving the furniture around was his way of working off the frustrations of his job. But finally my curiosity got the better of me, and I asked him why he kept changing things. "It helps my thinking," he explained. "When I look at the same old things, I think the same old thoughts, but when the furniture is changed, my thinking changes."

In the retail business, it was, and undoubtedly still is, the habit to rearrange the merchandise in a department to stimulate the sales staff and customers. The effect was to stimulate business, as merchandise that was old suddenly took on a new look when placed in a fresh location.

Well, that started me thinking. The creative geniuses of our culture tend to be noted for their erratic lifestyles. Whether because of natural temperament, economic deprivation or contemporary political upheavals, our great composers, painters and poets have been creatures of irregular hours and unpredictable habits.

Could it be that every habit we develop to make our lives easier or more efficient actually stifles our imaginations? Routine is the enemy of creative thinking. The challenges of new ideas, of fresh juxtapositions of objects in our personal environments, force us to explore the realm of possibilities and come up with fresh solutions.

Most of my medical friends agree that keeping busy and working with unfamiliar problems is salutary and tends to prolong life. Until she died at ninety-seven, my mother was an advocate of those very ideas and practiced them assiduously. I have followed and find that they work well for me too.

When I retired from the retail business several years ago, I set myself up as a consultant in marketing and customer service. I avoid assignments that are repetitions of previous experience and try to concentrate on those that are new and fresh to me, calling for research in areas beyond my previous experiences.

Like playing the piano, creative thinking might be a skill that the more we exercise, the better we develop. So to keep the little gray cells in top form, we should rescue our lives from thoughtless habits.

Keeping Friendships in Repair

"A man, sir," said Dr. Samuel Johnson, "should keep his friendships in repair."

A few years ago, when I first encountered this sagacious counsel, I made up my mind to turn back the clock regulating my life and determined to recapture some friendly relations of earlier days. Obviously, it was easier to reestablish some than others; a few had gone to seed, and others had drifted too far downstream. Those were in the minority; most responded to the challenge to revive common interests.

One man whom I had not seen in twenty-five years was suffering from cancer; he hadn't seen anyone for the past five years who wasn't in some way related to his disease. He was visibly grateful to be able to talk to an old acquaintance about happier years of his life.

Another was a distinguished woman author who lived in a remote upstate New York village. We had corresponded intermittently for the past dozen years, so I decided to pay her a visit. My efforts were rewarded amply by her reactions. She had been unable to travel because of severe arthritis, so she was cut off from most of her old associates and from the outside world. She responded positively to my suggestion that she assemble a group of her unpublished short stories, which I took to her publisher, who plans to publish them next year.

I found that people who undergo illness or reversals of fortune often get lost from their social community. When such individuals become self-conscious, they detach themselves from old relationships, and sometimes their friends are guilty of letting them slip away into oblivion.

In the early sixties, I was visited by a young British writer, Roald Dahl, who had spent some time in Taylor, Texas, and had met members of the White family of the well-known Scott and White Clinic. I had read some of Dahl's short stories and introduced him to Alfred Knopf, the publisher, who shared my enthusiasm and promptly became his publisher.

On a recent trip to England, I decided to drive down to Buckinghamshire, fifty miles outside of London, to renew our acquaintance. It proved successful for both of us and was well worth the effort. I was able to help him catch up on America, which he had not visited in a dozen years, and he brought me up to date on his more recent writing.

There is nothing heroic about looking up old friends; it is just the application of the Golden Rule, which carries its own reward. This, in part, is what Dr. Johnson was referring to in the quotation cited at the beginning of this piece. I suspect also that he meant that no effort should be spared to relieve promptly any friction between friends that might lead to a deterioration of the relationship. Oftentimes, all that is needed is a simple telephone call and an apology. The words, "I'm sorry," work wonders.

 The Decline of the Insult

An essay in *Time* magazine noted the demise of the skillful insult, "a result," it said, "of the death of confrontation in general." *Time* hasn't seen the confrontations I have!

Confrontations are alive and well between two ladies who wear identical dresses to the biggest social event of the year. Salespeople in fine stores have always tried to keep ladies who went to the same parties from buying the same dress, but occasionally their skills go for nought. Most often, the duplicated ladies laugh it off and compliment the good taste of each other.

Sometimes, the sight of one's dress on another woman would sharpen otherwise gentle tongues. One beautiful young matron, on seeing a rival walk in wearing an identical thousand-dollar gown, shrugged, "Oh well, that's what I get for buying a cheap dress off the rack!" Another lady, confronted with a twin dress, drew other guests' attention to the different accessories that her rival wore. Then she all but hissed, "I'm always so interested in what other people find attractive."

But the naughtiest insult I ever heard fly between ladies appeared to be totally unmotivated by anything but simple ill will. At a large charity ball a dowager lost an extremely valuable diamond and ruby earring on the dance floor. Everyone began to look for it. In the sudden silence that resulted, an impatient voice rang out in exasperation. "Well, it's no wonder you lost it! You've had your face lifted so many times you have no earlobes left!"

H. L. Mencken, the iconoclastic essayist of the twenties, held the record for brevity in his barbed replies to unsolicited letters of complaint. A favorite was his reponse to a woman who complained about what he had written. It read, "Dear Madam. You may be right!" Another of equal sharpness read, "There may be much in what you say, but not very much."

One of the wheeler-dealer oil men of the thirties made a historic insult in court when he was on the stand against a former partner. The opposing attorney kept pressing the oilman for a comment on the character of the plaintiff. He tried to avoid answering but finally, after the fourth request, he replied, "My former associate has all of the characteristics of a cur dog—except loyalty!"

Perhaps the insult reached its peak during the days of dueling. With the disappearance of this lively activity, the number of insults seems to have suffered a severe decline.

Wit, subtlety and style are the essence of the telling insult. These days, women seem to have a greater abundance of these qualities than do men.

Looking May Not Be Seeing

Most of us are blessed with good eyesight, but too frequently we look without seeing, discerning or remembering. Years ago, I used a system which had amazingly good results in improving my own observation and that of my children.

It is very easy to see a painting and fail to recall that it is a composition containing two apples, a pear, a teapot, a teacup, half a loaf of bread and a bowl of sugar. We settle with the impression that it is a fruit picture, and we judge it by the whole rather than its components.

For a long time, I have followed the practice of memorizing every element in a painting, closing my eyes as I mentally recall each one, then looking back at the painting to see what I had failed to remember. It is surprising how this exercise actually will expand one's retention of objects seen.

This practice helped me in my business because I was able to remember details of a hundred garments I would see in a New York or Paris fashion show, much more than most of my colleagues or competitors. It enabled me to spot objects in a cluttered antique shop in Hong Kong to the point that one of my associates dubbed me "the man with vacuum cleaner eyes." It forces the act of seeing as opposed to the act of looking.

When my children were eight and ten, we played a game at the dinner table that required them to look at a picture and then, with back turned to the painting, recount what they had observed. The one who recalled the most elements or objects received a small prize. It increased their powers of perception and enabled them to improve their retention of what they had seen. It must have impressed them, for I noticed the other day that they are conducting similar games with their children.

One of the greatest teachers in learning to look and see is Reinhold Marxhausen, a retired art professor in a little college in Seward, Nebraska. More important than the art he taught was how he taught students, workers and businessmen to see commonplace articles that surround them—things they had ignored for a lifetime. He opened new doors of vision for me. Actually, that is what real artists do every day; that is the essential difference between them and those of us who are not artists. They learned to see at an early period in their lives; we didn't.

In tribute to this great vision instructor, the citizens of his town recently honored him with a celebration which bankers and farmers, doctors and mechanics attended. Marxhausen contributed to my ability to see; the least I can do is to admit my indebtedness to him and to sing his praises.

Eyesight is one of our most valuable human faculties, but we are apt to take it for granted until it becomes diminished or lost. My greatest hope would be that art teachers around the land would learn the Marxhausen system and would teach their students to look and see.

# Why We Like Critical Critics

As a longtime reader of the critics, I have been wondering lately why they seem to be so much more respectable when they condemn than when they praise.

It's not just the critics who garner more respect when they pan rather than praise. It happens to all of us at any party we may attend. Mention that you hated the latest book, movie or art show that the critics acclaimed, and you will draw a crowd who cannot wait to hear why you boldly swim against the tide.

Obviously, your tastes are so refined that you are offended by what even the elite find to be admirable. But suppose you like what the critics are united in calling tasteless. Nobody gasps at the depths of your audacity. Indeed, nobody even asks why you disagree.

Your fellow guests quickly edge away from you as if they want to be out of hearing range before you say, "I may not know anything about art, but I know what I like." They gleefully speculate that you must have a velvet painting and watch television reruns of *Let's Make a Deal.*

This attitude is particularly mystifying when we consider the fact that time often proves immediate judgements wrong. Great artists achieve immortality regardless of contemporary opinion, while critics are generally remembered only for their spectacular misjudgements. It requires more courage to take the stand of praising something than it does to criticize it by nitpicking and spotting the invariable defect.

Criticism has its rightful place in society—whether it is right or wrong. It establishes a beachhead of opinion on which the firepower of those who disagree or concur can be directed.

Action begets reaction. If we don't agree with the critic, it forces us to develop an opposing point of view which in itself can be subject to attack. If we agree, our egos are rewarded by the alignment of our opinions with those of the critic.

Perhaps the reason why there is so much adverse criticism today is that the critic hopes to assure his place in history by sooner or later panning whoever becomes our twentieth-century Shakespeare.

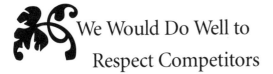# We Would Do Well to Respect Competitors

I don't want to second-guess the Bible, but I sometimes believe we would be better off if—instead of commanding, "thou shalt not covet thy neighbor's ox"—it had ordered us to "honor thy competitor."

For the most part, we Americans do not covet our neighbor's ox. Since we still persistently believe in the American dream that if we work hard enough we'll have our own ox, we do not begrudge others the enjoyment of theirs, unless it appears they happen not to be American.

A few years ago, a group of Japanese businessmen bought the Haworth Country Club in northern New Jersey. They then raised the membership fee from $300 a year to over $5,000. Older members complained that the higher fees were discriminatory, since only those in the affluent Japanese community could afford them.

"This is a classic case of how bigotry is created," *The New York Times* quoted an old member as saying. He went on to complain, "I've always admired the Japanese people for creating a great society and culture on a small island, but all of a sudden, I find that I don't like them." Another old member said he's frightened "because outsiders—Arabs and Japanese—are coming in and buying things up and pricing Americans out of the market, making us second-class citizens."

The irony of the situation is inescapable. For generations, we have been exploiting the resources and buying up the best that Europe, Asia and Third World countries offer, disliking them because they are not like us. Now that they've become formidable competitors, we dislike them because they are just like us. First, we are inclined to blame newcomers to our midst because they are unlike us; then as they copy us, our complaint shifts to the blame that they are imitating us and competing with us. Obviously, we cannot have it both ways.

As a retailer, I learned that the best way to deal with competitors was to work with them toward some larger goal beneficial to us all. As a result of that practice, many of them became friendly. We discussed that what we had in common was more important than what we had in conflict with each other.

On Acknowledging Gifts

We Americans are noted for our ability to get things done —except when it comes to writing thank you notes. This national procrastination may have come with the territory.

Since I am an inveterate letter writer, prompt attention to thank you notes never has been a problem for me. Indeed, I have long made a practice of writing a note of appreciation to actors for performances I have enjoyed or to writers for books or articles I have admired, whether I have known them or not. I have been more than rewarded for my time by new friendships and experiences the habit has brought me.

If you cannot seem to get around to setting pen to paper, you may find comfort in a curious custom I ran across recently in a short story by Oliver La Farge, the great Southwestern anthropologist. The Hopi, an ancient tribe of Pueblo Indians who live in the arid northeastern corner of Arizona, are rich in tradition but poor in material goods. Among them, a gift requires acknowledgment just as surely as your Aunt Ellen expects to hear that you loved her hand-knit, lime green necktie. According to La Farge, however, a Hopi would consider the immediate acknowledgment of a gift to be unspeakable rudeness.

The gift must be fully savored and all of its facets explored before the giver can be properly thanked. The greater the gift, the longer this process takes and the later the thanks is delivered to the giver. A prompt thank you from a Hopi would show how slightly he regarded your gift.

Not only do gifts need to be acknowledged, but favors, large and small, and small acts of kindness or thoughtfulness are deserving of recognition. Brief appreciations, either on a post card or in letter form, are actually part of the accoutrements of a civilized culture.

I am constantly amazed at the lack of manners, not only of younger generations but older ones as well, for the failure of a recipient of a favor to go to the great trouble of taking a pen in hand to write a brief "thank you." Perhaps this dereliction can be traced to the general decline in letter writing, thanks to the ubiquitous telephone. In another ten generations, our thumb and forefingers, used to grasp a pen, may well have atrophied.

Writing thank you notes might be less odious if we would think of them as gifts themselves. Think of the pleasure notes will bring to someone who was expecting nothing more from the mailbox than bills and circulars.

Birthdays Fill a Special Need

Many of the pleasures of childhood should be part of adult life as well. Whatever our age, we need to play, to lie under a tree thinking long, deep thoughts, to experience the excitement of learning—and have our own special day. I am referring to the anniversaries of our birth.

Birthdays are important for children. Having a special day set aside during the year is a fine way to help a child gain a sense of being a unique individual. Who can forget that vast gulf of time adults called a year that loomed between these marvelous days? Then it was a month, then only a week, and the big day arrived that was ours alone!

Some time after we had grown old enough to drive, to vote and to marry, birthdays got a bad reputation. Jack Benny invented that awful joke of being thirty-nine. Birthdays became unpleasant reminders that we were drawing closer to that undesirable time of useless old age.

That's too bad, for a couple of reasons. For one, we are beginning to lose our prejudice against aging. For another, we never outgrow our need—at least once a year—to feel special. I don't advocate public celebration. I discourage my family and friends from making a fuss over my birthday, but I love to savor in private that special ebullience I feel that no accumulation of birthdays seems to diminish.

When I was young, I was convinced that I could not be a survivor: I knew that I would not live to see my fiftieth year. At that time, I did not realize how smart I had been to have picked parents with such good genes.

Perhaps it's because my birthday comes in the spring, a time when I am surrounded by reminders of nature's own rebirth. The blossoming redbuds, azaleas and fruit trees decorate my birthdays with breathtaking bouquets whose beauty more than offsets any depression I feel at being a year older. I learn anew that life itself, older than civilization, is forever young.

Since birthdays are important to each individual, it is also important for friends to recognize the occasion by a call or a card. It is the act of remembrance that is important. We all want to know that we have made sufficient impact on others to be worthy of remembrance.

I was a child of five or so when my mother told me that every day was somebody's birthday. "Every day a birthday!" I thought. "The world must be a wonderful place!" Part of me has never grown up, I suppose, because I still think so.

1988

A Modest Scientific Solution

For years, there has been an informal debate going on as to what is best for our school kids. Should they pray? Should they have sex education? Should they read books with dirty words in them?

There have been a lot of opinions, but there have been no facts, because there are no facts. Why not find out, once and for all? Paul Simon once sang, "it's all happening at the zoo"; nowadays, the arena in which we play out the drama of our time is the classroom.

Proponents of school prayer say it is the salvation of individual morals. Opponents say it is the damnation of individual rights. Proponents of sex education say ignorance of such matters leads to teenage pregnancy and promiscuity. Opponents of sex education say knowledge of such matters leads to the same thing. And on it goes. Neither side convinces the other, nor will they in a million years.

We pride ourselves on the fact that we are living in a scientific age. The scientific method is to make conclusions on the basis of proven facts and not on emotion or conjecture.

The way things are now, we have no rational or scientific basis on which to base our decision. All we have is a mass of opinions divided down the middle. Let's eliminate all this speculation and put scientific methods to work. Starting now, for a period of two generations, let's enact legislation limiting childbearing to exactly two children. One child will receive sex education and read any books he or she likes. Then in twenty years or so, we will take a look at how they developed. There would be no distortion because of environment, heredity or economic status.

Fair is fair. Whichever side turns out the best adjusted, morally upright, socially adept and productive kids gets to have things its way for the next generation. That way, our leaders and lawmakers could concentrate on the minor issues facing us, such as pollution control, waste disposal, disarmament and alternative energy sources—just in case there is another generation.

Admittedly, I am trying to combine the judgment of King Solomon and the irony of Jonathan Swift. We need the wisdom of both of those gentlemen to remind us that our concern for our children's morals might better be replaced by a concern for their survival.

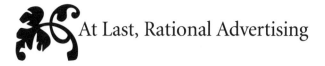

At Last, Rational Advertising

Several generations have been raised on advertising hyperbole that lures buyers by the use of such words as "the cheapest," "the best," "the finest." Often these ads are illustrated by men jumping into the air to demonstrate their exuberance caused by the superlative proclamations that have been used to describe the product.

Little is said in the advertising about the ingredients of the products or the manufacturing techniques that make the articles "better." Little emphasis is directed to rational motivation, perhaps because emotional appeals can be expressed in smaller space in the print media or less time on television. Perhaps the advertising profession believes that the mass market responds more positively to emotional appeals than those directed to reasonable considerations.

Thus it was refreshing to see an advertising blurb in a recent book printer's catalog that read:

> To make work better for its purpose than was commonly thought worthwhile was D. B. Updike's goal at the Merrymount Press, and it is ours as well. We give the same care and attention to any printing job, large or small, quaint or grand. Working with clients who appreciate fine materials, hand craftsmanship and attention to detail, we endeavor to produce printing that will satisfy the discriminating eye.
>
> Each kind of printing has its particular challenges: from letterheads, to menus, to pamphlets, to posters, to programs, to books of 400 pages, we *like* what we do. We combine enthusi-

asm with our skills so that printing is our pleasure as well as our work. It's your money and our time; we might as well enjoy spending them both!

Wouldn't it be exhilarating to read an automobile dealer's appeal to his customers with a similar message? Or to learn of a clothing store that expresses a philosophy acknowledging the importance of satisfying "the discriminating eye"? Or a florist who acknowledges that "we *like* what we do"? Or a stationer who proclaims, "We embrace enthusiam with our skills so that printing is our pleasure as well as our work"?

Wouldn't any business, large or small, benefit by the establishment and enforcement of an operating philosophy embodied in the sentence, "It's your money and our time, we might as well enjoy spending them both"?

Customers are yearning for more and better service from intelligent salespeople who understand their jobs and their products. They are willing to pay a price for satisfaction, a quality that is so hard to come by in this era of mass production and mass distribution. They are frustrated by being treated as consumers when in actuality they are customers. *Consumer* is a name originated by a marketing genius to describe a statistical abstraction. *Customer* is a living human being.

What's in a Business Name?

Since consulting is my business, I receive a number of requests for advice. Some are simple queries for an opinion or a sense of direction, such as one by a friend who is about to open her own business. She has experience in her field, a sound business plan and adequate financing, but she still had an important decision to make: what to name it.

"I'm looking for a name that means the best or the pinnacle of its kind," my friend said. "All I can think of is 'Hallmark,' and that's taken."

"There are a number of words to describe your concept," I told her, "such as 'Acme,' 'Superior,' 'Best' or 'A-1,' but these are so old-fashioned that they've become cliches."

There are fashions and fads in business names, just as there are in clothes and children's names. Around the turn of the century, people named their businesses after themselves: Proctor & Gamble, Brooks Bros., Tiffany.

You can always spot a business started in the do-your-own-thing late sixties and seventies. The style then was cloying cuteness or puns, such as the "Able to Travel Agency" or "Lord of the Rings Engine Repair."

"That's just it," my friend said. "I don't want a name that marks my company as being an early eighties fad."

Another classic name style was informational, giving both the location and the nature of the business: the Elm Street Laundry, the Grand Avenue Bank and Trust, and Standard Oil of New Jersey. With the dawn of technology, fashion favored crisp, scientific-sounding names manufactured from syllables or initials: Conoco, Woolco, Batus, Pepsico. Such mode names have been favored by firms dealing in new inventions or chemical concoctions, but indications show that synthesized names like Allegis, Unisys and the like are proving to be somewhat unintelligible to the public, with the result that the trend is back to the forthright use of the principals' names.

The exceptions are those companies willing and able to put millions of dollars behind the establishment of such names for years on end, such as Exxon. With enough money, any name, good or bad, can be made into a household word.

It is not the name that makes or breaks a new business. It is the quality and value of the product and the integrity of its service, plus its financial strength to hang on during the first few years of growth.

My friend made a sound decision by naming her business after herself. In this day of impersonalized conglomerates, it's a good way for the smaller business to signal to its potential customers that it has an owner who is waiting to provide them with a maximum of personal service, before and after the sale.

# We Can Play It Too Safe

The baby boomers are about to have their midlife crisis. I was alerted to that by a conversation I had the other day with my friend Rick, who is among the vanguard of those already past forty.

"I wouldn't mind so much that we only go around once," he said to me, "if I could just be sure I would get all the way around."

At first I thought he was kidding. He is a textbook yuppie: advancing through middle management of a well-run company where he is highly regarded; married to an intelligent beauty who has her own career; possessor of a BMW and other trappings of the good life; handsome and in such good condition from bicycling and proper diet that his cholesterol is probably measured by a negative number. Yet Rick believes life is passing him by.

Thinking back, I realized that when I was Rick's age I felt I already had "been round" at least once, having lived through a full measure of challenge and accomplishment. Now, when I consider the rich merry-go-round of my years, I must have been around so many times I should feel absolutely giddy. But Rick feels he may be cheated out of even one full ride. What makes the difference? I think it might be our attitudes toward risk.

People of my generation grew up taking risk for granted. We remember the killer childhood diseases, worldwide depression and at least one world war. But as these threats disappeared, so did our tolerance for risk. We began to pass laws that went beyond forbidding outright danger, to those that attempt to keep us out of potentially harmful situations, such as banning cigarettes in public places—and from potentially harmful decisions, such as "cooling-off" provisions before strikes are invoked. This overconcern for our skins and our psyches has delivered the wrong message to Rick and his fellow boomers. Perhaps we have taught them to play it too safe.

Rick has succeeded at everything he has attempted. To others, that means he is a success. But he knows better. He knows something is missing from his life, and he feels cheated because of that lack. What he lacks is risk—taking a chance on something that he was not sure up front that he could do. It is our stretching and reaching—and sometimes failing—that rounds out our lives and makes us feel complete. I have always liked the line from William Blake's *Marriage of Heaven and Hell*—"You never know what is enough unless you know what is more than enough."

I am not advocating jumping out of airplanes or taking up bullfighting. I am talking about a different kind of courage—the kind it takes to start your own business, to send your manuscript to an agent, to apply for a job beyond your present qualifications, to learn a new skill, to reach out to new people, to do whatever it takes to get your life going again when it seems to have stalled out on you.

So if you are afraid you are one of those who is not making it all the way around, try taking the kind of risk I am recommending to Rick. It won't be a smooth ride, but I guarantee you will know you have had the complete trip.

# Gifts That Outlast the Marriage

Love, as the song goes, may be twice as nice the second time around, but to those of us who are expected to take a gift to the wedding, the repeat wedding presents a problem. Unfortunately, we don't get any credit for the beautiful ceramic vase or crystal wine glasses we gave on the first occasion.

The dilemma we face, when confronted with the celebrants of a second marriage, is becoming so widespread that I asked some social researchers to address the issue. They have used the best poll-taking techniques, including personal encounters, telephone calls and written questionnaires.

The statistics indicate that the twice- or thrice-weds are likely to possess already every toaster and candlestick they will need for a lifetime, so we are faced with the problem of what to give those who already have everything. Even if you know them well, it is hard to determine what tangible goods each of the partners is bringing along to the new union.

The consensus of the individuals interviewed was that the happy couple should be given something of a consumable or otherwise temporal nature, such as a bottle of fine wine, symphony tickets or several hours' use of a limousine.

There are countless things in this category that we never think of in terms of wedding gifts, such as caviar, a year's supply of saltine wafers, a gift bond for dry cleaning or lawn mowing for an entire summer.

As my friend Gerry Stutz, the former president of Henri Bendel, summed up, "The gifts should be something you know the recipients will enjoy, but will be gone in a few hours." I think this advice is right on target, except that it is turned exactly around.

Why give the tea service and the candlesticks to the first-weds when statistics show their marriage might tarnish before the silver? There would be far less pain during the inevitable split if the divorcing couple had to divide only the memories of a smoked salmon or a dozen roses rather than the heirloom samovar, Baccarat crystal or a set of Crown Derby demitasse cups. That would leave the wedding guests a choice of the traditional gifts for a second marriage, with rather more assurance that the gifts won't outlast the marriage.

Along with the bride's choice of silver and china, perhaps bridal registry services could post the odds for the marriage's survival. If this practice were legalized, betting on marriage successes might give the horses and dogs a race for the money, thereby fattening our public coffers. The more stable-appearing the match, the more permanent could be our choice of gifts. Revenue hungry legislators should take heed of this so-far untapped source of tax revenue.

If more people were interested in the outcome of marriages, perhaps they would last longer. The cohesiveness might be provided by the enlargement of the number of people betting on the outcome.

# White Collars Turn Blue

More often than not, our dealings with those white collar workers designated to service our needs result in more frustration than service. Could it be because technology is turning our white collar workers blue?

Ever since the end of World War II, people have been predicting the changes in our lives that would be brought about by the new technology. One of the more accurate forecasts was that our manufactured goods economy would be replaced by one based on service instead. However, what nobody thought about was that the same technology that automated our factories would also automate our services. In other words, our white collar jobs are turning blue.

I need to define my terms, so there can be no misunderstanding. Let's call a blue-collar job one that involves the manipulation of machinery and a white-collar job one that involves the manipulation of the mind. As a result of the computer revolution involving word processors, electronic filing systems and automatic inventory controls, office and clerical workers are increasingly called on to punch the proper button instead of tracking information in their heads.

There are great benefits to these new processes: freedom from drudgery and speed, for example. But we are beginning to see the negative aspects as well. Some of our frustrations with salespeople who don't sell and who don't know their stock can be blamed on technology, I think. We have replaced true salespersons with button-punchers who need to know only how to punch in the inventory and credit card numbers and the transaction price so that all is well with the computer.

All of this sounds so magical, and some computers actually are, such as the non-time-consuming ones used by the food markets. They alone, of all retailers, have learned how to handle a customer at the checkout counter, read eighteen prices from the bar codes, pack all of the items in sizes as diverse as a watermelon and a fresh haddock, sack them and say, "Thank you—come again," all in the matter of 123 seconds.

An order of that same complexity would delay a customer in any department store eleven and a half minutes at best, and even then the buyer probably would have to go to the credit department to clear a charge account that contained the purchases of Aunt Sue and some joker from across town with a name remotely similar. No wonder many customers are yearning for the old-fashioned cash register that actually rang instead of whirring.

Computers are wonderful inventions, but their buttons extract only stored facts. They cannot handle the daily situations where the deal is clinched or the situation saved because somebody cared enough to do some independent thinking. So far, none of the great computer makers have come up with one that can be plugged into an ear or stuck in the mouth to determine if the customer has been satisfied.

# Kool Aid Firing Squad

Analog foods, or foods that look and taste like natural foods but are really synthetically manufactured substitutes, are gaining popularity in U.S. food processing. In the Soviet Union, however, making artificial foods is a crime. Recently, a manufacturer of fake fruit juice was put to death by a firing squad. His crime? Selling bogus fruit juice consisting of water, sugar and additives, but no real fruit. This could be one of the few cases in history of a man being killed because of false advertising. In the U.S.A., a similar practice rated only one year and a day's sentence, plus a $100,000 fine. That was the punishment meted to two top officials of the Beech-Nut Company a few months ago.

We in America are obviously more tolerant about the artificial things we eat and drink. We are not critical about advertising that makes a big deal out of a brand of fruit drink containing only ten percent natural fruit juice. As a matter of fact, that ten percent juice is usually portrayed in packaging and advertising as being superior to another brand that is 100 percent artificial.

We seem rather blasé about claims such as those of a chip manufacturer that say, "now made with more real cheese." More real cheese than what? A deck of playing cards? More real cheese than a baseball bat? Who knows?

The ironic thing to me is that what this guy was selling sounds more like what we give our children on hot summer days than something that's so heinous. Then, again, maybe real fruit . . . and real cheese . . . should be something that we expect rather than being a *luxury* or an *additive* to a synthetic product. I would hate to be the one to suggest such a strong penalty for the manufacturer of analog foods, but when you begin reading food labels and the only natural ingredient appears to be water, you do recognize the necessity of strong government supervision of food products and the importance for stepped-up enforcement programs.

It was not too many years ago that Italian consumers were stunned by the revelation that some cheese makers were mixing marble dust with cheese batches to increase the weight, and adding ox blood to red wine to give more body to the beverage. The culprits pleaded guilty but excused themselves on the grounds of "ameliorata"—making things better!

Perhaps I could take a cue from the advertisers of analog foods and package myself like this: "This column has been made with ten percent factual information, five percent perspective, and improved with a dash of wit." Would Russian editorial writers get shot for a comment like that?

 Media Discovers Schools' Woes

Now that the National Commission on Excellence shares the public's concern about education, it would be easy to assume that better schools are on the way, but in the words of *Porgy and Bess*, "It ain't necessarily so."

One of the quaint customs of our country is that we don't take anything seriously until it appears on the covers of *Time* and *Newsweek* or gets Dan Rather's undivided attention for two minutes on the evening news. Then it becomes what we call a "media event," whereupon we shower it with such minute attention that we get bored to death with it and can't wait to go on to the next thing.

Such a fate has befallen the plight of our schools. Anguished parents, concerned employers and the shortchanged students themselves have been questioning our school system for at least a decade, but largely had been swept aside until the recent massive publicity made the problem fodder for the politicians and the media.

Now it qualifies for the "quick fix," the magic solution derived after fifteen minutes of soul-searching during an "in-depth" analysis on a television news magazine show. There are already several possible quick fixes vying for our support. Among these are elimination of the so-called social pass, return to the three R's, crackdown on classroom drugs, establishment of school prayer, and merit pay for teachers.

This latter one is the most popular solution, since it involves a dissenting labor organization, something politicians and press alike cherish for its potential to generate more controversial headlines than concrete progress.

Comparing American education statistics with those of Japan and Europe can be discouraging and embarrassing. We don't show up well at all. I am inclined to put the blame not only on our school systems, but also on the shoulders of the American parents who are unwilling to accept the proposition that education is a joint responsibility of the home and the school district.

The opposition to Texas's no-pass, no-play rule is evidence of the fact that too many parents regard football prowess and baton-twirling skills as being of equal or superior importance to the mastering of chemistry and history.

Solving our public education problems can happen only through long term commitment, untainted by selfish goals of the various special interests and parents. Unfortunately, that seems to be the only thing our can-do country won't do.

When Golden Rule Fails Us

The Golden Rule, "Do unto others as you would have them do unto you," is a time-honored code of ideal behavior. There is one everyday area of our lives, however, where its effectiveness breaks down.

It's no wonder that the same philosophy that formulated the Golden Rule also asserted that it is more blessed to give than to receive. Sometimes, it is hard to be grateful for gifts that have been chosen with the Golden Rule in mind: that is, when we are given something that the giver would personally like to have. Too often the taste or the recipient's needs fail to coincide with the benefactor's.

For years, I thought I was just being overly critical, but in checking around, I learned the problem is not unique: everyone has had similar experiences. A mother of grown children says she dreads gift-receiving occasions because she knows her daughters invariably will send her china, silver and other accoutrements of formal dining. Just starting their own households, the daughters require such things. They never seem to wonder what their mother will do with them, even though she turned her dining room into a potter-workshop years ago.

The executive who prides himself on his contemporary office suite is given rococo pen wells while he reciprocates with equally unappreciated memberships in the museum of avant-garde art. The sports buff gets the complete works of Arthur Miller and wonders why his hockey tickets are cooly received. The chronic dieter gets chocolates while he gives his skinny friends gift certificates to the health spa.

In all other instances, the Golden Rule works well. It helps establish comfortable working relationships in school, business and marital life. Mark Twain, when asked about the relative merits of several religions, is said to have replied, "There's nothing wrong with Christianity—if only people practiced it." The same pithy comment would apply equally well to all other religions, as well as to the Golden Rule.

Some shrug off inappropriate gifts by saying, "It's the thought that counts," but if the Golden Rule giver did any thinking, he would notice that the interests and requirements of others are sometimes different from his own. What is needed is more and better thinking by the gift donor about the interests and lifestyles of the recipients.

The next time there is an occasion to select a gift, try putting yourself into the recipient's shoes, skin or psyche. Try saying, "If I were Mary and were twenty-seven, what would I want or need; if I were Tom, thirty-two and struggling to support a family of four, what would brighten my day?" The answers come loud and clear when posed in this manner.

1989

The Real Problem of Aging

Now that the Baby Boom generation is approaching middle age, we hear a lot of talk about the graying of America. Those of us who are a little further down the road have some tips on what you can expect.

The worst thing about getting older is not wrinkles, balding heads, stiffening joints or slowing systems. The truth is that most of us are as healthy as ever and feel just fine, thanks. The only reason we give a second thought to wrinkles or hair is because you youngsters are so smug about your own smooth skin and silken tresses. You'd be surprised how many of us like the way we look.

No, the real curse of increasing age is reading glasses. Just when you get to the point where you realize that minutes are precious, you have to spend a lot of them searching for your reading glasses.

You thought it could never happen to you, but inevitably you come to grips with that old gag that your arms are simply too short to get the telephone book in focus.

Once you resign yourself, you schedule a trip to the ophthalmologist, who sends you to the optician with a new prescription. You choose a pair of frames that your friends assure you make you look as dashing as a ski instructor in dark goggles.

After all, reading glasses are a wonderful prop. You can take them off and wave them grandly to make a point, or you can slide them down your nose and peer over them menacingly, or as benignly as Kris Kringle.

But just as you're thinking they are not so bad after all, you start misplacing them. Not even dedicated joggers cover as many miles as you do looking for your specs.

It's no good having an extra pair. You immediately lose both of them.

If you don't lose them, you sit on them in your car seat, step on them in your bathroom or roll over on them when they slip off as you doze off for a nap.

Your grandchildren find them to be fascinating playthings which twist so easily as they grab them from your nose. Pet dogs even relish the flavor of mock tortoise specs as they chew on a pair left unguarded.

An ingenious engineer should be able to develop spectacles with a built-in beeper system that would increase in volume as you get hot on the trail of the elusive glasses, or get fainter as you get farther away.

That's not too much to ask in an age when a man was put on the moon and a machine grinds coffee beans and perks the coffee at exactly 6:45 A.M.

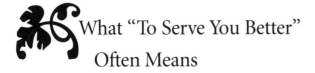# What "To Serve You Better" Often Means

Have you observed the growing frequency of a phrase that often accompanies your favorite products or appears on the monthly statements of your charge accounts? I am referring to that apparently innocuous notice, "to serve you better." Do you know what it really means?

"To serve you better" on a soft drink bottle often means that the price has gone up at the same time the deposit has been eliminated, or that the bottle size has been decreased. As Betty Cook pointed out in *Dallas Life*, "The 'to serve you better' boys are sneaking behind most private doors." She was writing about the installation of pollution-free electric hand dryers that are being placed in many public restrooms.

In such areas, there are usually signs that read, "These devices are built to protect you from the hazards of disease which can be transmitted by cloth towels or paper towel litter. This clean, quick, sanitary method dries hands more thoroughly and prevents chafing." I question the validity of this statement, for I've found that these electric blowtorches leave my hands chafed and damp.

In most instances, "to serve you better" is an excuse for a change in policy relative to a product or customer service that has become uneconomical to the product but is still desired by the customer. It has gotten to the point that whenever I see a sign that says, "to serve you better," my suspicions immediately are aroused. I have a strong hunch that I am being taken under false pretenses.

The "new and better" label across a box of laundry soap or cereal oftentimes is a signal that the price has been raised or that the size of the box has been decreased, a practice which Andy Rooney has commented about on *60 Minutes*. "New" is regarded as a magical word that carries with it the privilege to increase the price of a product. Seemingly, the use of "new" is designed to suppress any protest or complaint. Interestingly enough, it is rarely used to introduce a lower price.

A quality that has all but departed from our life today is candor. By now, the public has become aware of the forces of inflation that push prices up, as well as wage increases and changing value of the dollar that have the same effects. Why don't manufacturers and retailers quit being cute and tell us straight out, "We're sorry, but increasing costs force us to reprice our products"? Frankness would be respected and accepted as a matter of fact.

There is nothing wrong with justifiable price increases or the installation of labor-saving devices for more economical operation. I just don't want to be soft-soaped in the process.

Society Functions on Faith

The taxicab's radio blared forth the horrible account of the mass murder of the schoolchildren in Stockton, California. The announcer concluded with the comment, "Investigations reveal that the mass murderer who finally shot himself was a drifter with a long record of incarcerations in mental institutions over the nation. Can parents send their children off to school with any degree of certainty they'll see them again alive?"

The cab driver turned back to me at the stoplight and said, "Not any surer than I am able to guarantee you safe passage from the airport to your hotel."

After such horrible incidents, it is not uncommon for humans to question their ability to have faith in anything. It's bromidic to comment on the vagaries of life, but hazards are part of the basic nature of life, and there is little we can do other than exercise reasonable care. We can buy insurance against death but not for the preservation of life. We are forced by circumstances to accept much of life on faith, however skeptical we may be. I am not referring to a faith in religion or in a supernatural power; I am speaking of faith in our fellow humans.

Our daily lives are built on our confidence in those with whom we live and upon whom we depend for myriad interactions and services. For the most part, they seldom let us down.

The man who proclaims he has lost faith still sits down in a barber's chair and is often shaved by a barber he has never seen before and most likely will never meet again. All of us put our lives in the hands of those we don't know and who are located in control towers hundreds of miles away. We trust the operating efficiency of a stoplight. These are supreme acts of faith. We express universal faith in the thousands of people who cook the food we eat at a restaurant or at a quick food counter or at a baseball park.

Every elevator ride we take requires faith that the inspector of the machinery did a good job in checking the condition of the cables and brakes. The same is true for every time we take our cars to the shop for repairs or even our shoes in for new heels. We should hope that the mechanics did their jobs properly, but we don't check; we assume they did. When surgery is required, we do not bring in an observer to supervise the procedures of the surgeon who is cutting us open, for we assume that he knows his business.

This does not mean that we are right. Perhaps we should be more demanding in the protection of our security, but the truth of the matter is that we have neither the time nor inclination to question all the possibilities of danger that threaten us. Experience has taught us that we can take much for granted. With all that does go wrong in daily living, it is surprising how much goes right. That is the basis of our faith.

Nonetheless, it might not be a bad idea to check the inspection expiration date in the elevator cab, the validity of our taxi driver's license, the health examiner's rating of the restaurant in which we eat. After all, it's our life!

There Are Reasons for Regulations

Left to our own choice, most of us, I believe, would prefer to live in an unregulated society, provided there would be no increase in the hazards to living.

Complete deregulation works well as long as there is only one person involved, but the instant the population is doubled, some regulation becomes necessary, even though the rules may be self-imposed. As the number of inhabitants increases, the village, town, city or state has to step in to establish regulations and a method for meting out the penalties for violators.

Those of us who have lived for a long period of time are, perhaps, more aware of the need for societal rules of conduct because we've had the chance to observe the abuses that occur when a society attempts to live on an honor system.

Here are a few specific cases that are worthy of examination.

Why shouldn't an individual have the right to design and build a house exactly as he wants without interference from a building inspector who insists that it be constructed in conformance with the city code? Restrictions weren't necessary as long as there was just one homeowner. The minute there were two, ten, fifty or five hundred, each of those homeowners had a concern about the manner in which any neighboring houses might be built, for each house threatened every other one as a potential fire hazard, pollution source and garbage producer.

This scenario suggests the conditions that developing communities faced that led to the regulations known as building codes.

A similar situation occurred when automobiles proliferated,

creating traffic and safety problems. These hazards led to the establishment of speed laws, driving rules and, eventually, automobile licenses.

The failure of landlords to regularly examine the elevators in their buildings resulted in cable and brake failures, and the loss of lives forced municipalities to enact regulations and periodic examinations of elevator equipment.

Anyone with any degree of interest in human life would recognize that the employment of young children as factory workers would imperil their health and interfere with their education. There were so many exploiters of children that it finally took a constitutional amendment to eliminate child labor.

These incidents illustrate how regulations came about. In the course of making regulations, our legislative representatives have made some mistakes. In some cases they have been guilty of over-regulating, setting the stage for Ronald Reagan to declare war against all regulations and regulatory bodies and to deregulate everything in sight.

This was a classic case of throwing the baby out with the bath water. In some instances, Mr. Reagan's deregulations will stand; in many others, regulations will have to be restored because a complex society cannot run on an honor system, nor can it expect industries in a profit-motivated economy to be judicious enough to regulate themselves when there are financial advantages at stake.

The deregulation of the savings and loan industry will be forever a black mark on the record of Mr. Reagan. This deregulation, in which Congress was a participant, is a shocking and costly example of the abandonment of common sense for which the taxpayers will pay and pay and pay. For that, taxpayers will remember both of them forever—and not fondly.

Salespersons Becoming Endangered

It may well be that salespeople are on their way to becoming an endangered species. So many stores have reduced their sales staffs that you might have already concluded they are extinct.

One of the retailing words I most dislike is "clerk," for it has the connotation of an order-taker—no more, no less. A "salesperson," on the other hand, is one who assists, offers solutions to problems, answers questions and provides help.

When I was active in retailing, I used to meet with salespeople regularly, and constantly reiterated my concept of a salesperson's function.

If what a salesperson does is to hand the customer the exact article requested, that is not selling; that is order filling. And it can be done by a vending machine more efficiently than by a human. Besides, vending machines do not chew gum or have bad breath.

The art of selling, on the other hand, requires imagination—to visualize the customers' needs and requirements, to exhibit a knowledge of the stocks of goods available for sale, and enthusiasm for the products being sold.

A professional salesperson has an understanding of the prospective buyer and how the quality of happiness can be projected by a smile, by body language, by a tone of the voice.

We want to be "sold." None of us wants to be oversold; that is the worst kind of selling. Most of us appreciate the skill of a professional in sports, theater, music and selling—whether it be in stores, automobile showrooms or on TV.

The height of professionalism is illustrated by the effortless swing of a Jack Nicklaus when he drives the ball 350 yards down the fairway, by the easy bowing of violinist Isaac Stern in concert, by the skilled salesperson who has the knack of finding just what we want in a minimum amount of time.

Professionals make the hard things look easy. A professional salesperson knows where the merchandise is located, what's in stock, what's coming in, what will meet your needs, what won't.

Customers do not have time these days to deal with salespeople in any field who are amateurs, who waste time, who are more concerned with their commissions than with the buyer's benefits.

A good sales organization is nearly always the result of an enlightened management that chooses its staff with care, educates it with diligence, supervises it constantly, compensates it fairly and rewards unusual performance by understanding that human beings live not by bread alone.

The Effects of Merger Mania

The results of the trend toward mergers and takeovers are apt to be felt by different segments of our economy in a variety of ways. The lawyers who are putting them together are having a field day financially and are obviously pleased with the results, as are the investment bankers who have made millions and sometimes billions of dollars from merger activities.

Employees have fared less well as companies begin to constrict their staffs in order to provide funds for increased interest charges. Staff shrinkages result in less service for the customers, who are already dissatisfied by the lack of adequately experienced personnel, so the mergers are not good for customers.

Finally, the communities at large are likely to pay a heavy price as corporate headquarters are moved from Dallas, Miami and St. Louis to Tokyo, New York and Frankfurt. Local corporations historically have provided the backbone of support for the cultural, educational and health activities of our cities. The local merchants, bankers and manufacturers traditionally have been the ones to back drives for the enrichment of the cultural and educational life of their cities. As residents of the community, they were familiar with the legitimacy of institutional needs and ambitions. They aided the campaigns with both leadership contributions and manpower.

Since merger mania, the scene has shifted. A local request for funds to support a theater drive in Louisville, Kentucky, is likely to be passed on to the new corporate headquarters a thousand or more miles away, where it will be scrutinized by a management committee that knows little or nothing of Louisville's distinguished accomplishments in community theater.

My guess is that many drives are going to come up short in the years ahead unless big business reviews this problem seriously and with a high sense of urgency—before blight occurs.

As anyone who has participated in fund-raising knows, momentum is vital for the success of such endeavors. Volunteer workers are stimulated and encouraged by prompt pledges, just as their spirits sag when prospects are dilatory in making decisions.

This is not an attempt to beat a paper tiger, for as a fund-raiser, I have encountered such experiences in recent months. Nor is there an intent to ignore the generous support that many national companies make to the communities they serve. Too many of them, though, do not distribute their philanthropy throughout the nation, but tend to concentrate their gifts to cities in which their headquarters are based.

Ever since the 1935 revenue act that legalized corporate tax deductions of five percent of pretax earnings and the subsequent "Vanderbilt decisions" of the Supreme Court of New Jersey, ruling that a corporation has the power to make reasonable charitable contributions, corporate leaders and boards of directors have felt comfortable in directing part of their earnings to support community endeavors.

Only a few spirited corporations, though, have seen fit to follow the example of the Minneapolis business group, headed by the Dayton Hudson department store, to allocate five percent of pretax profits to philanthropic causes.

As governmental bodies are forced to curtail budgets, the greatest hope for survival of the arts is through greater national corporate participation in their support. Institutions like Philip Morris, American Airlines, AT&T and American Express, among others, have set a splendid leadership pattern.

Katherine Anne Porter, the distinguished novelist, wrote, "The arts outlive governments and creeds and societies, even the very civilizations that produced them. They are what we find again when the ruins are cleared away."

The Decline of "Luxury" Goods

A lead article in the business section of a recent issue of *The New York Times* carried the headline "Luxury Cars Lose Some Status," with a quote from a spokesman for BMW who questioned, "Have our cars ceased to be status symbols? It's a serious question."

Serious it is for all expensive products, including cars and evening gowns, diamond necklaces and sable coats. All of these commodities depend on the maintenance of a mystique that is based sometimes on relative rarity, but always by the acceptance of those in the "know" who recognize quality and taste and who understand the difference between "better" and "best."

This is a question to which every maker of luxury goods needs to find answers, for the future of expensive, high-quality products may be at stake. There is a need to find the facts and take action before erosion has set in too deeply.

In the nineteenth century, deluxe, top-of-the-line products were made by hand in small quantities for a restricted market of very wealthy customers. Demand for top-quality products increased in the twentieth century, reaching a peak in the "spending seventies" and "egocentric eighties." The increase in number of high-income buyers forced the manufacturers of deluxe goods to adopt mass production techniques to meet the expanded demand.

Makers of dresses and automobiles produced reasonable facsimiles of the deluxe goods for the new-to-the-market customers. This was satisfactory for a time, but soon the sophisticated customers began to realize they were not getting the genuine product, but were being offered instead "a reasonable facsimile thereof."

Handwork was replaced wherever possible by hand-operated machines; finish was determined by the limitations of both the machine and the supervising management, which had limited experience in meeting the exacting demands of sophisticated customers. The production system has become an impersonal one in which the worker has lost the opportunity of hearing customers' reactions and criticisms directly.

The nineteenth-century artisan who dealt directly with the customer was educated and motivated by the exacting demands of his most critical customers. Today those demands are transmitted from the salesman to the buyer, who relays them to the manufacturer's sales representative, who sends them to the sales manager, who finally conveys them to the production manager, who may or may not convey the critique to the workers.

The drop-off in sales of expensive import cars may have been the result of "a growing number of people regarding lavish spending as socially irresponsible," as *The New York Times* reported, or, as I suspect, it may well be that the products just aren't as good as the buyers expect for the price being asked.

Conspicuous consumption may be in decline, but the demand for finely made products in all fields is greater than at any time in world history. The markets sometimes get confused and produce ornate, expensive products that are ostentatious and lack elegance.

Our industrial system, which is based on translating expensive goods to lower-price categories, requires finely made experimental products created for a wealthy market, so that the successes can then be made for less critical customers at substantially lower prices. The acceptance or rejection of the top quality goods gives the mass makers direction for future production.

These customers at the top of the economic order will pay the prices of such goods only if they are convinced that they are getting superior quality. If, however, they are offered a handbag or a steering wheel made of die-cut commercial plastic instead of leather, then they think twice.

If a pair of shoes made in Italy selling for $350 is made of the same quality of leather as a similar style made in Greece that sells for $165, then the former is going to suffer. This example has its analogies in dresses, sweaters, automobiles, handbags and other fashion products.

Quality is, of course, more than superficial appearances. Methods of construction assure satisfaction and provide longevity for the product. Customers are aware of hidden values and are willing to pay for them if they are receiving aesthetic gratification as well.

Our copyright laws on fashion design in the U.S. are weak and difficult to enforce, so the top-priced article is often copied by the "look alike" producers at substantially lower prices. Therefore it is incumbent on the better maker to build intrinsic value in construction (to make the product look better, feel better, run better, last longer) as well as in aesthetics (to make it please the eye, look distinctive, please longer).

No longer do the labels "Made in France" or "Made in Italy" cushion the impact of overpriced goods. That is a plus for goods made in the U.S., but the lowered value of the dollar is a serious negative factor in the price vs. value relationship. That becomes the big challenge for American producers to overcome. The dollar won't always be down, but by the time it changes, domestic makers of fine products may be down and out.

# Maybe We Are Getting Better

On West 52nd Street in New York, I saw a bit of graffiti on a wall that read, "This is the sum of all our lore. We never learn better, we just know more."

There is plenty of evidence to support this view, but there is also a case to be made against it.

Even though I have lived through the great Depression and two world wars, I have to admit that the 1950s were my least favorite period in history. We had just finished two decades of winning wars. We were so self-congratulatory and sure of ourselves, so patronizing in our victories, so full of muscle from our self-righteous use of the atom bomb, it's surprising that many of our more mature neighbors on this planet could tolerate us. We were so busy beating our own drums that we could not hear the faint hymns of appreciation for our largess.

This period was followed by two decades of losing wars, rioting cities, and rebelling children and sexes. This experience has taught us some hard lessons and, I hope, turned us into more tolerant, thoughtful human beings.

At least this is true of science, I learned when my fascination with the Voyager space probes sent me scurrying for a new text-book in astronomy. I had not looked into one since the fifties, when the text recited so-called facts—in the same self assured way that characterized the rest of that pompous decade—such as Saturn having the only rings in the solar sytem, only one of many errors Voyager has uncovered.

144

The new textbook was a big surprise. In the first paragraph, I read, "Any scientific law is constantly subject to refinement as we accumulate new data. Nor is science the only path to truth. Art, music, literature and science are different, but all contribute to our understanding of the human experience."

For the most part, the rest of the world admires the United States, and in many instances we are actually liked. The quality of self-righteousness that we cultivated so assiduously and unconsciously irritated people in many lands. They recognized and appreciated our achievements, but they knew we were not as good as we thought we were.

Modesty was never one of our most noticeable qualities, despite presidential efforts to lead the bragging brigade. But as individuals and the country grew older, they developed penetrating abilities to evaluate the foibles of youth.

If the textbook I mentioned is typical in its message of open-mindedness, tolerance and appreciation for other philosophies, then there is indeed hope that we humans may be accumulating more wisdom, not just more facts.

Trimming the Deadwood

Although I am an advocate of sitting back and letting nature take its course, there is one gardening chore I enjoy thoroughly, and that's pruning. I guess it is my retailer experience that encourages me to get rid of old stock as well as deadwood.

There is something about pruning that satisfies my soul. No matter what kind of day I've had, I always cheer up when I assault an untidy tangle of undisciplined branches and reveal the efficient, healthy growth it conceals.

I delight in cutting off an unproductive branch here and there or a limb that is going in the wrong direction. Its dead weight threatens the roses below. My pleasure is undiminished even when the wood removed is an unpleasant reminder of things outside my control, such as damage from storm or disease. Or perhaps it is the victim of my own poor planning, such as planting seedlings too close to each other, with the unforeseen consequences which show up ten years later. There is no use bemoaning them. It is far better to direct energy toward ridding the tree of overlapping branches so that both can thrive.

I suppose my zeal is reflective of the hard-earned lessons I learned as a retail merchant. My mentors proved to me that nothing would revive dying merchandise, and that the faster you moved it from your stock the more quickly you would have funds to reinvest in fresh stock that provided the opportunity to make a profit. I learned through experience that if the dress that looked so great in the showroom dies on the sales rack, lop it off to make room for the new.

I think a readiness to prune is a good way to approach life, too. Those who live to the fullest do not wait for the dead branch in their lives to blow off and rip a hole in their new convertible before they make a needed change. I am referring to ritualized habits no longer having a meaning to one's contemporary life.

Pruning can be too deep in personal life or in foliage. I am for trimming out the deadwood to encourage new growth, not chopping down the whole tree.

 Cocktail Party Problems

One of my pet peeves is the large stand-up cocktail party, where the noise level is many decibels higher than a basketball game, the hors d'oeuvres scarcer than Super Bowl tickets and the drinks weaker than the hitting power of baseball pitchers. Aside from the booze producers, the ear specialists and the makers of hearing devices must be the only beneficiaries of the modern cocktail party.

Our culture certainly is capable of inventing a more satisfying entertainment function than the cocktail party. Born of Prohibition, it has become a standard device for paying back social obligations, introducing new product lines, recently promoted vice presidents and redecorated headquarters.

No one can take it as a compliment to be invited to one of these demonstrations of gregariousness where clichés float around aimlessly and dangerously, chests become belabeled and backs get slapped.

Wouldn't it be refreshing and memorable to receive an invitation that read, "Suspecting that you, too, dislike large cocktail parties, I'm sending you a baguette of French bread, a block of ripe Brie cheese and an assortment of alcoholic beverages so that you can enjoy them sitting down in the comfort and privacy of your own home. All of this is in honor of our newly elected vice president, Sylvester Scrimshaw. He's a lovely guy, and I think you will enjoy meeting him on some other occasion when you'll both have time to have a decent conversation."

With an invitation like that, I don't think I would ever forget Sylvester Scrimshaw, and I would go out of my way to meet him.

The big cocktail party has even infected the small cocktail party where there is ample seating. So used to standing at large parties, guests follow the same practice at intimate home affairs. If the Lord had meant for man to stand while drinking, He surely would have created a third foot to the rear to provide man with a tripod.

Many of society's ailments can be traced back to bigness—big business, big tomatoes, big cars, big heads, big unions, big schools and big cocktail parties. When things get too big, they do not function so well, taste as good, relate to society as smoothly.

But, coming back to cocktail parties, I have noticed a particular thing. I find not only that liquor goes down just as well when seated but that the quality of conversation goes up as well. Try it sometime. You'll like it.

There's a Better Scare than Horror Movies

Even though I don't watch them, I am aware that horror movies continue their popularity; the bloodier, the better. Recently, I read that a psychologist defends the gore because it provides the viewer with needed stimulation.

Whether we want to be or not, we are all exposed to TV previews of horror movies. We know that entire high school graduating classes are wiped out by knife-wielding maniacs, and honeymoon campers are felled—like the forests—with chain saws.

The classic argument of those who defend the genre is familiar. Ever since Aristotle, critics have told us that it's good for us to be scared out of our wits by make-believe. We are purged of our fears by the restoration of order at the end. No sooner is the stage littered by the bodies of Hamlet and most of his kin than Fortinbras and Horatio say, in effect, "Well it was a mess; but things will be all right from now on."

Just so, are we supposed to leave the theater with a sigh of relief that it's not us dismembered in a trunk on our way to Chicago? William Shakespeare made his point without the graphic splashes of blood and rolling heads of today's horror movies. Surely, that can't be good for us. Not so, says the psychologist. Human beings need a certain amount of stimulation, and the butchery of horror movies provides it, he says.

Even the century-old Sicilian puppet shows, based on the legends of the Crusades, are ended with battle scenes in which the conquering Crusaders lop off the heads of the Moors, much in the spirit of the modern western.

150

Assuming it is true that we all need an occasional shock to keep us from turning into carrots, surely the least imaginative of us could think of a more constructive way to turn on the adrenalin.

Bullfights in the Latin countries and the popularity of wrestling and boxing matches in ours meet the psychological demands for stimulation, as do gang movies on TV, and televised football and basketball games. Viewers with a known heart condition are well advised to have a vial of nitrostat at hand when watching the bodily contact sports.

If you think your life could use more stimulation, join a public speaking club, compete in a sport, overbid your bridge hand or, better yet, start your own business. I guarantee that's a never-ending series of shocks.

Clothes Can Make a Difference

In the immediate postwar period, my associates and I had to spend a considerable amount of time in Europe in search of new manufacturing sources. We traveled by train to cover the short distances between towns we were visiting, and to pass the time in the crowded train compartments, we devised a game which we called identity. Each of us was allowed three minutes to determine the other passenger's country of origin by some detail of clothing he or she was wearing.

Some of us got pretty good at this, for at that time clothes were not as internationalized as they are today. One glance at the shape of the toe of a man's shoe or the thickness of the sole would be sufficient to label him not only Italian, but northern or southern Italian. The shape of a shirt collar would identify its wearer as French, and the necktie would almost always give away a Spaniard or a Greek. Women proved to be more difficult, but we found other clues to be able to include them in our little pastime.

That was then, but now, forty years later, clothing has become so homogeneous that it gives no evidence as to the homeland of the individual: it will reveal only the country in which the article is made.

All of this is by way of setting the background for an observation I want to make about the growing internationalization of clothing. I am not referring to the passing of quaint, historical costumes that the women of Bruges or Normandy wore on certain occasions, or even the festive costumes of Greece and northern Italy.

The clothes I mean are those that are worn by government officials in Russia and Poland, by street people in China, by financial tycoons in Hong Kong and Hawaii. Western dress has become the accepted order of the day in almost all places except Iran, where the attire is as reminiscent of the past as is the thinking of its leaders.

In the course of the last half dozen years, Western garb has become the accepted accoutrement for men and women. The ubiquitous T-shirts and jeans probably started the stampede, but now all of the amenities are being observed: neat neckties, Italian spread collars, double-vented jackets and the licensed designer apparel for women, together with their Vuitton or Gucci bags bought in the Singapore airport or from street vendors on Fifth Avenue.

Whether this is good or bad, I dare not pass an opinion, but this is a subject that sociologists and psychologists might want to consider. By adopting the apparel fashions of the West, do they infer that they are prepared for our social, economic and governmental habits as well? Does this switch-over presage an abandonment of their time-honored habits and mores? Are they prepared for the possible consequences, and are we?

One thing, though, becomes apparent, and that is that fear breeds on differentness. When our citizens saw Soviet leaders in baggy clothes and babushkas, it contributed to our evaluation of them as being unlike us. We even had difficulty in believing that they did not want war any more than we did. Now, when we see a smartly dressed Soviet delegate to the congress, we say to ourselves, "He looks like us; he must be like us—good and kind. We aren't too different, after all."

People may not have changed, but our evaluations of them can be influenced by a necktie.

Is So-called Self-fulfillment Really Greed?

A recent poll said that sixty-three percent of adult Americans are searching for self-fulfillment. Only sixty-three percent? Why not 100 percent? Maybe self-fulfillment doesn't mean what I think it means, so I have looked up the definition.

The word is in my dictionary right between self-fruitful and self-generated. If anybody asks for a definition of "self-fulfillment," it is accurate to say it means the act of fulfilling one's ambitions, or, in essence, to be satisfied with one's life. One would think that everybody would want a satisfying life, so if only sixty-three percent are still looking, that would mean that thirty-seven percent of us are already satisfied.

Think of ten of your friends and concentrate on the four you think are most contented with their lot in life. Aren't they still trying to lose ten pounds, eliminate their crab grass or make the duplicate bridge team? So, "self-fulfillment" must mean something else. I am not up on the jargon of pop psychology. The last book on the subject I read was *I'm OK; You're OK*. I figured if we were all OK, then there wasn't much more to be said.

Judging from the deluge of similar books since, I guess I was wrong, but I felt that it was "OK" if I didn't read them. To correct this lack, I've been investigating articles that deal with the notion of "self-fulfillment." It most often appears in connection with the "me" generation, which was the one that came right after the gapped generation. In these articles, "self-fulfillment" is touted as a positive value to be sought in preference to such tiresome old negative values as self-denial, obligations to friends and family, and hard work. Do you suppose "self-fulfillment" is just a fancy new way of saying "selfishness"?

We have seen evidence in recent years that selfishness is being applauded as a national virtue. Pre-election polls indicated that many voters were planning to cast their votes on the basis of self-interest rather than for candidates espousing issues that were more valuable for the national good.

Wall Street, which has been a longtime scapegoat for our ills, is, in a way, a magnification of our national ethos. The callous and cynical attitude of some of the moneychangers finds itself replicated at local levels by the operations of many of the savings and loan operations which were directed to satisfying the needs of its executives rather than the public they were supposed to serve.

The distressing thing about this so-called self-fulfillment is that it belittles those who do find satisfaction in service to others, whether they're members of a community endeavor or just contented team players.

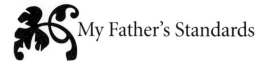 My Father's Standards

I was introduced to the retail business under the direction of my father. This was both a rewarding and frustrating experience, for he was a difficult man to satisfy. The standards my father set for his home and children were no different than those he established in his business. He had no tolerance for mediocrity. He expected the best; he got the best.

He was determined to improve the quality of all merchandise offered in his store and to present it with a maximum of personalized sales assistance. He was no snob about price, being willing to sell an article for $2 if it was good enough to be sold for that price, or $20,000 if it was good enough.

His approach to merchandise was constantly: "How can we make it better? What will the manufacturer do to improve the product if we pay him more money?" He never tried to knock the price down, for he knew from experience that every time the manufacturer decreased his price he took something out of the quality of the article. He was determined to sell merchandise that was as free from flaw as possible.

He stated his position very carefully when he said, "As retail experts, we know more than the customer; therefore, it is our obligation to eliminate any flaws in the product before it gets into the customer's hands."

To that end, he established an inspection department, unique in the retail business, in which every article of apparel was tried on a model form to determine if it was cut properly and if there were any defects apparent on close inspection.

In my years of retail experience, no one has ever returned a product because it was too fine or too beautiful. Customers are like Oscar Wilde, who said, "I have the simplest of taste. I'm easily satisfied with the best."

Defending the Bill of Rights

Ever since the Supreme Court decision on flag desecration, it has been interesting to observe not only the public's reactions to the ruling but those of public officials, as well, including the President and assorted political types, educators and the press, including columnists, sportswriters and the editors of the obituary pages.

I grew up in the belief, impressed on me by parents and teachers alike, that one of the glories of being a U.S. citizen was the political freedom that citizens of our country enjoy and which are guaranteed to all—black, white, brown or purple—by the Constitution of the United States and particularly by a series of amendments to that remarkable document known familiarly as the Bill of Rights.

After writing the Declaration of Independence and the Constitution, the signing fathers came to the conclusion that they had omitted some essential assurances, so they proceeded to add ten amendments to tidy things up and to give the citizens an improved package of benefits. Over the intervening years, there have been attempts to tinker with these amendments, but public opinion has successfully defended them against efforts to curtail the freedoms guaranteed in many of the articles.

In the current attempt to change Article 1, relating to the abridgement of freedom of speech, it appears that many patriotic citizens have permitted their emotions to overcome their common sense.

Even President Bush yielded to the opportunity of pre-empting the United States flag and draping it around himself so completely that he has claimed it as his personal political property and has made it difficult for anyone disagreeing with him to speak freely in support of the Supreme Court's decision in the case of Gregory Johnson. President Bush has assumed the role of a national cheerleader and weakened his position as our national political leader. He has failed to lead the country to a clear understanding of the issues at stake, but has responded to public outrage by proposing an amendment that could weaken the cherished guarantee of free expression.

I found the flag burning act of Mr. Johnson distasteful, but I think that he harmed himself and not his fellow citizens, past or present. Patriotism is the veneration of a country and its philosophical principles; not necessarily of its songs or flag or any related symbol. We give our lives to fight for our country and the privilege we possess as citizens.

If the proponents for an amendment feel so strongly, why don't they include the prohibition of the usage of the flag for any purposes other than on the battlefield or its display on federal and state buildings? Why don't they prohibit it from being used for lapel buttons, decorations for conventions, product advertising, chorus girl costumes, shoulder patches for nightclub security guards and replication by the Navajo Indians?

Alex Burton, a columnist for *City Life*, writes, "How many tattered flags do you see hanging or fluttering from flagpoles? Is that any way to treat a flag?"

I yield to no man in my dedication and loyalty to my country, but I am dismayed when its elected chief executive officer attempts to convert an unpopular Supreme Court decision into next year's congressional campaign issue. The president of the United States should be above such political opportunism.

Another Good Lesson in Retailing

Several weeks ago, I wrote about the most satisfying sale I ever made. Here is an account of the hardest sale I ever made—one that involved killing a $5,000 sale that I had just made and replacing it with another at $795.

Several years after I started work, I was given the responsibility of buying for and managing our very small fur department at Neiman Marcus. One day my father came in to examine the stock, and he came across a beautiful black broadtail coat that was priced at $5,000. The coat had been in stock for about ten months, and my father reminded me that if we did not sell it before Christmas, we would have to reduce it substantially in our annual fur sale. His parting advice to me as he left the stockroom was, "You'd better find a customer for this coat."

A few days later, he came on the floor and saw me having the broadtail coat fitted on a customer. He called me aside quietly and said, "What are you doing?" I replied, "I am doing what you told me to do. I've just sold the coat to a customer." He said, "You are making a mistake."

"Why?" I asked. He replied, "Because that lady sells insurance, and whenever she comes into the store, you may notice that she carries a big leather portfolio filled with policies she's delivering. As she walks, you'll observe that her right arm with the envelope is rubbing against the front of her coat. In no time, this broadtail coat will be devoid of fur."

"I've taken care of that," I said. "She understands that it is very fragile fur." My father in his wisdom said, "Yes, I know she understands it now, but she won't understand it the day the fur is worn off. You're making a mistake in selling her that coat. You'd better go back and sell her another."

As a dutiful son, I went back and unsold the $5,000 coat and sold her instead a durable Hudson seal coat at $795 that she wore with great satisfaction for seven or eight years.

When our clearance came after Christmas, we did mark the coat down to half-price, and we sold it to a woman with a chauffeur-driven car and several other fur coats. She wore her broadtail coat with great satisfaction for seven years. This was concrete evidence that my father meant what he said when he stated, "No sale is a good sale unless it is a good buy for the customer." He was willing to take a loss rather than sell a fur coat to the wrong person.

This policy is in no way heroic; it is pure common sense. If a dealer sells a product that satisfies, the customer comes back; if he sells one that fails to meet expectations, then in a free society the customer goes elsewhere for subsequent purchases. It is so simple that it is surprising so many sellers have not learned about it.

Serendipity Is More Than Luck

The word "serendipity" is frequently used, but I doubt if many are aware of its origin; the history of the word and how it came into usage is interesting.

It first appeared in a book by Horace Walpole, an eighteenth-century English writer who wrote in a letter to a friend, "I once read a silly fairy tale called *The Three Princes of Serendip.* As Their Highnesses traveled, they were always making discoveries, by accident and sagacity, of things which they were not in quest of. For instance, one of them observed that a mule, blind in the right eye, had traveled the road lately, as evidenced by the fact that the grass was eaten only on the left side."

A commentator on Mr. Walpole went on to explain, "Serendipity, thus, immediately is defined as the gift of finding, by chance and by sagacity, valuable or agreeable things not sought for. It is not an 'either/or' phenomenon, but both accident and sagacity have to come in while one is in the pursuit of something else. Thus 'accidental discovery' is not a synonym for serendipity."

Once when I was visiting an artisan's studio in a small village in Italy, I came across a box full of silver thimbles decorated with semiprecious stones which had been stored in a cabinet. The maker said he had put them away because they were too difficult to manufacture. Finally, I was able to cajole him into producing enough for us to feature in our Neiman Marcus Christmas catalog, after giving him a substantial order for more profitable silver punch bowls. The thimbles, which retailed at that time for $5, proved to be a great success. They were fine enough to send to a grandmother or a duchess. As a matter of fact, one was ordered by a customer as a gift for a princess.

That was a case of serendipity; other examples are bountiful. When people are in the right place at the right time, they reap rich rewards unrelated to effort. Those who have had the good fortune to find oil on a sun-parched ranch or in the back yard of a nursery may be considered to have been "lucky," or beneficiaries of serendipity. A book collector picking through racks of old books in search for a first edition of John Steinbeck's *Grapes of Wrath* discovered an autographed letter of George Washington's—far greater in value than the book for which he was searching. A blind date arranged by a third party may in some instances have a serendipitous ending—a happy marriage.

There is enough evidence of serendipity in life to suggest that we not knock it.

Will Collecting Be a Lost Art?

Escalated prices of artworks have removed paintings and sculptures by established contemporary artists from the reach of average collectors. Furthermore, the prices of most art collectibles eliminate all but the super rich from the collecting field.

When I first started collecting in the thirties, it was possible to buy pre-Columbian Mexican terra cottas for under $100, oil paintings by unknown young artists for under $500, posters for $5 and ballplayer cards for fifty cents.

Not only have prices vaulted out of reach, but supplies of many collectibles have become exhausted. Genuine antiques, in marketable quantities, from colonial Mexico and South America are non-existent; antiques from India are a thing of the past; pre-Columbian pottery and textiles from Latin American countries are, for the most part, illegal to export; early American glass has been gobbled up by the museums, together with early American furniture, quilts and artifacts. "Collectibles" has become a marketing classification, and spurious, limited editions of ceramics, etchings, silver reproductions and other decorative objects are now being manufactured for people who have money to spend but who possess little knowledge.

With only the dregs of European and English antiques on the markets, furniture and decorative pieces from the mid-fifties are becoming the antiques of today. Desk lamps that won prizes in the Trienniele at Milan in 1939 and Fornasetti painted metal desks and screens from the sixties are seen frequently in the Christie and Sotheby auction catalogs. Throwaways of our generation are now amongst the collectibles of the future.

Nineteenth- and twentieth-century collecting was centered in great part on the household decorations of the Victorian period, which was the first historical period that mass manufacturing had supplied. The fine handicrafts such as lace, embroidery and inlaid wood started to disappear from the market as manufacturing took over production in the latter part of the century.

The question of what is going to be left to collect in the year 2010 often receives the answer, "Oh well, there will always be something that collectors can find."

That is not a conclusive answer, for prices may be so high, based on scarcity, that fewer people can be expected to acquire. The other side of the coin may be availability, which may restrict collectors to objects that are within their art budgets.

There are few areas that twenty-first century collectors may have to explore: stuffed animals and mounted fish, many of which have survived attic storage; Rolls-Royce ephemera, such as hood ornaments with the Rolls-Royce insignia, may be the only affordable items connected with that famous name; old picnic hampers; hand-painted Victorian and Edwardian envelopes that may have survived interment in the files of their British recipients.

The year 2000 A.D. may very well be labeled as the beginning of the century of paper in which letters, brochures and ephemera that have not been self-destructing may be the only things left with any inherent and affordable value to collect.

Publishing Can Be a Miniature Venture

When I was a college senior, I had a compelling desire to become a book publisher, but my father strongly urged me to go into retailing instead. I yielded to his importunities and never had cause to regret my decision to accept his advice.

In my second career after retiring from retailing, I finally became a publisher by starting the Somesuch Press. Since publishing can be costly, I went into it in a small way, by issuing very small books, miniature books, which measure not more than three inches in height.

Why would anyone want books that small? Well, actually, there are not too many people who do want them, but there are small groups of collectors scattered all over the world who collect these tiny books. Napoleon Bonaparte did. Franklin D. Roosevelt was a collector, as is the present queen of England.

Miniature book printing started shortly after Johann Gutenberg printed his Bible in the fifteenth century. Some contemporary must have seen it and commented to himself, "If Gutenberg can print a great big book, I'll show him that I can print a very tiny book." Then another printer who saw the tiny book declared that he could print one even smaller, so the race was on.

Actually, there is a very good reason for small books in the seventeenth and eighteenth centuries, when people traveled by stagecoach. Seating space was so crowded that a big volume would have been impossible to open without having part of it fall into the lap of a fellow passenger. A small book secreted in the waistcoat pocket must have been a great convenience in a crowded carriage.

Most of the early books were devoted to religion-related subjects, both for adults and for children, such as maxims from the Bible, the catechism and rules of proper conduct for young boys and girls.

Miniature books have been printed in almost every country in the world on a wide variety of subjects, ranging from poetry to horsemanship. In Hungary, with no tradition for miniatures until after World War II, there developed a sizable industry for making such tiny volumes.

Postwar shortages forced the Hungarians to teach printing in their trade schools in miniature form to stretch out limited supplies of paper and ink. These books were sold at modest prices, and, as a result, there developed a prolific audience of Hungarian collectors, who may number as many as 18,000—more than in all of the rest of the world combined.

Today's miniature book producers are scattered all over the world, but the predominant number of them seem to be centered in the United States. For the most part, these publishers operate private presses located all over the country with a predominance in California. Many of the books are hand set and printed on imported paper, thus putting them into the category of fine press editions.

Can such small books be read by a person with average eyesight? That is the ultimate test, for a book that isn't legible has no more justification than any automobile without an engine.

 1990

Mail Order, not Male Order

During my career as a retail merchant, our store received numerous unusual requests from customers. We delivered a pair of ducks across the country as a gift from a doting grandfather to his grandson. We climbed the rocks of the Pacific coastline to fit a mink coat on Elizabeth Taylor. But a letter from a lady in Tennessee proved to be the record breaker.

The writer stated she was a widow and was in search of a male companion between seventy and seventy-five who was completely and absolutely finished with sex. Being familiar with our reputation for being a store that never refused any request, she was turning to us in desperation to fill this order.

From time to time, we had been bombarded with challenges to supply baby elephants, coats made from exotic yarns or furs, archaic recipes and fighting cocks. We had an order for a life-size Snoopy two days before Christmas that required delivery to be made without fail in Athens, Greece, on Christmas morning. We met the specified time with two hours to spare, but never had we been asked to locate a male companion for a lonely woman.

Our mail order department was perplexed as to how to answer the customer and asked if I would write to her. It was a difficult letter to compose, but finally I came up with this reply: "Not that we shrink from a challenging task, but since all of our services carry a satisfaction guarantee, I'm afraid the risk for us is too great, particularly when your specifications are so precise and rigid.

"Frankly, I wouldn't even know where or how to search for such a man, nor do I think I would believe him if I found him, nor would I recommend that you put too much faith in any man who claims to meet your requirements."

The kind of loneliness that impelled her to write to us is only too real for thousands of men and women who for reasons of shyness, fear of rejection or the inability to meet other unattached people find themselves alone and anchorless. This condition undoubtedly explains in part the large number of publications that do a thriving business by carrying want ads for personal contacts.

I concluded by advising her, "Get interested in a hobby, or join a local club devoted to your interests. In all likelihood, you'll meet a man who will share them. Thanks for writing to us with such confidence. We do a large mail (M-A-I-L) order business, but we've never filled a male (M-A-L-E) order."

Our Contradictory Impulses

Sigmund Freud, faced with what he thought were irreconcilable contradictions in his female patients, cried, "What do women want?" I would not be surprised if our new budget-conscious administration were crying, "What do Americans want?"

We Americans are a contradictory tribe. When we are in an automobile, we run each other off the freeways at an alarming rate. But if I can catch your eye, you'll let me in ahead of you at a traffic jam.

As a nameless group, we demanded with our vote a reduction in welfare spending. The administration responded with budget cuts and tighter qualification rules. Then we cringed with outrage as the television networks and the news magazines unearthed examples of "worthy poor" who had fallen through the safety net.

Faced with impersonal numbers and our own tight budgets we demand an end to welfare cheats. But we don't ask for financial statements when the house down the street burns—we feel fortunate that we can help from our own blessed plenty.

It reminds me of a relative of mine, a crotchety old codger who never missed an opportunity to rail against public charities such as the United Way. He prided himself in never having given any of them a dime. Since his death, three young people, all orphans, have come to me separately to say, "He put me through college but made me promise not to tell." In public, we hold that we can't afford a welfare state. Privately, we wouldn't think of letting a child go hungry.

It is no wonder that the administration is confused. It gave us what we said we wanted while we all forgot that as a nation we cannot stand to ignore suffering. Finally, we are having to face the fact that we have to make some hard choices.

Despite ex-President Ronald Reagan's conviction that the homeless street people accept their condition out of choice, there are thousands of citizens who disagree with that idea and are putting up private funds to take the homeless off the streets and give them a new chance in life.

The vast majority of Americans cannot enjoy the warmth of their own homes while witnessing the unfortunate street dwellers.

It seems clear to me that what Americans want is to continue to assist our needy. Once we agree that it's our will, surely we are smart enough to figure out a way that is economically feasible.

# FDR's Missed Opportunity

Even now, 108 years after Franklin Delano Roosevelt was born, we have all been remembering, with varying degrees of approval, the history-making things he did. However, there was at least one thing that he did not do that he should have.

Whether we admired him or detested him, I think we all agree that FDR was a giant of a man who left the world irrevocably changed from the way he found it. Whether or not we agree with how he used his power, we agree that he was a powerful man in a powerful position. I happen to be an admirer of Mr. Roosevelt's, and I think he made wise decisions more often than not.

One choice he made, however, disappoints me. Although he was paralyzed from polio in his prime, he chose to conceal the fact as much as possible. We never saw then, nor do we see in newsreels now, evidence of his disability. There is rarely a trace of a wheelchair, leg braces or crutches in our images of this great man. Indeed, I know men and women who were children during the Roosevelt years who learned of his paralysis only years later from their college history courses.

It is easy to understand FDR's reluctance to display his handicap, and the courage he showed in ignoring it is nothing but admirable, but what an opportunity he missed! Had he but allowed it, his wheelchair, leg braces and crutches could have been as much a trademark of his indomitable spirit as his big grin and his cocky cigarette holder.

Far from being symbols of helplessness, these accoutrements might forever more remind us of one who could and did change the world. Whether it was personal vanity or the prevailing political wisdom, he and/or his advisers chose to camouflage his physical disability.

Those of us who lived through the years of the Great Depression recall the repetitive crises that he and the country faced, and the encouragement he gave to his fellow citizens as he attempted to find solutions for ailing banks, Dust Bowl sufferers, the unemployed and paralyzed industry.

He was praised by the majority and cursed by the minority for the money he threw at the problem. His critics claimed, "He will break the country." The truth of the matter is that the hundreds of millions he poured into the National Recovery Administration and the other alphabetical agencies was insufficient to pull the country out of the economic slough into which it had fallen.

Much as he spent, he did not spend enough. It was only when billions of dollars were appropriated for war preparations, leading to a full employment boom with overtime pay, that we moved out of the Depression.

We no longer have to fear paralysis from polio, but disease and accidents still confine some youngsters to wheelchairs. They should understand that physical disabilities cannot stop them from growing up to be president.

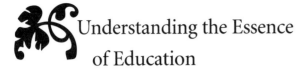Understanding the Essence of Education

Tough budgets and the obvious failures of our school systems are causing us to re-evaluate our philosophy of education. Just what is education, anyway? Naturally, most of us think we know.

Although I learned a wide assortment of facts, accumulated the required number of college credits and finally earned a degree, I received my true education in just one course. I did not realize at the time what an influence a Shakespeare survey class could have upon me.

My professor assigned what the students considered to be an unreasonable term paper. We were required to select one of the Shakespeare plays and search out all the scholarly criticism that had been written about it for the previous ten years. We had to read everything that we could get our hands on, even if it meant a trip to another college library.

Then we had to analyze our findings, complete with footnotes, which were considered to be burdensome busywork. Even a relatively obscure play by Shakespeare had been written about hundreds of times over a period of ten years. Nevertheless, if I did not do a credible job on my paper, I would not pass the course.

I chose *A Midsummer Night's Dream* and set to work reading as many expert opinions as I could find. It did not take me long to realize that some of my "experts" were illogical nitpickers and that even the best of them frequently disagreed. More learned Ph.D.s than you could imagine filled pages of journals with arguments over the size of Shakespeare's fairies or the phase of the midsummer moon.

I turned in my paper, passed the course and filed the experience in a remote corner of my brain. It was not until years later, when someone remarked on my skepticism about expert opinions, that I realized the influence that Shakespeare class had on my life.

Very few people would think that a course on Shakespeare could remotely influence a retailer's career or, for that matter, the career of a lawyer or a doctor. Nonetheless, all occupations are dependent mainly on the use of common sense, which on occasion has to be modified by expert judgment in related fields of inquiry.

The lesson I learned was neither to despise nor to accept blindly what the experts say, but rather to search out as many opinions as possible and then form my own conclusions. This, to me, is the essence of education.

In our television-influenced society, we are too apt to fall into the trap, described by Daniel Boorstin, former librarian of the Library of Congress, when he wrote in an essay, "To the ancient question, 'What is truth?' we Americans now reply, 'Sorry, I didn't watch the 7 o'clock news'."

Death Is Becoming a Stranger

Better health care and longer life expectancy mean that a generation of our population has grown up without close personal experience with death. This may not be entirely desirable.

A friend of mine in her early thirties recently confessed that she was morbidly afraid of death. Nobody she knew—relative, friend or even a casual classmate—had died. She feared her reaction to such adversity would be inadequate. At first I was surprised, but then realized that her experience might be the rule rather than the exception. When I was her age, I had experienced at least a dozen fatalities. Naturally, I am grateful that times have changed, but I am also glad that I understand that death is a part of life.

I remember when far-distant relatives, old friends and acquaintances of years ago gathered for a funeral. Sometimes, I'd meet grown cousins for the first time, gazing into eyes astonishingly like my own, and noting how my cheekbones and chin also worked in combination with blonde hair and olive skin. I could greet a favorite great-uncle and read my own future written in his weathered face. Old friends brought with them twenty years' worth of gossip; my contemporaries seeming to have aged incredibly while their parents were little changed from my memories of them.

The current emphasis on horror and violence in popular entertainment may be the result of this generation's excessive fear of the unknown.

It is difficult to generalize about any subject as mystical as death, but it seems to me that we accept more placidly than we did earlier this century.

Then, families, particularly the feminine members, went into paroxysms of grief when confronted with the loss of loved ones. There were days of tear-stained cheeks and grief-stricken brows that gave evidence of an unwillingness to accept the sad news. Families went into long periods of mourning during which virtually all social intercourse gave place to periods of mental self-flagellation. Colorful clothing was replaced by garments of sober hues, ranging from gray to black. Stationery and calling cards were edged with black borders, men wore black arm bands on the left sleeves of their suits, social participation was deferred for periods ranging from thirty days to six months, larger public appearances were restricted to a bare and absolute minimum, and women wore black veils over their hats to obscure the wearers' facial visibility.

I cannot say that death causes less grief today, but certainly our grandparents, with their more frequent exposure to death, took it much harder. Perhaps the explanation of this vast contrast in human emotions lies in the fact that our lives are busier than they were five decades ago; we have so many more claims on our time that there is just less time left over for overt grief.

Becoming an Ecologist by Marriage

Interest in the environment has been at the top of the agenda for lots of people for a long time, but I must confess that I tried to ignore the subject from an ignorance that made me resent people meddling in what I considered to be my own affairs. Now, I am a born-again environmentalist, having been influenced to open my eyes and mind by my wife, who proved to me that the world about us needed saving, if indeed we wanted to save ourselves. Hence, I am an environmentalist by marriage.

Formerly, I resented "do-gooders" telling me about the dangers of the garden sprays I was using on my property to eliminate bugs which were ruining my peonies. Now, I fault the chemical companies and their distributors who insist on marketing products that pollute the air we all breathe and who lobby our legislators so successfully that it is difficult to get adequate laws to protect the environment of the world in which we live and the people who inhabit it.

One day, my wife commented that she was giving an ultimatum to the pest control service that had served us for twenty years. "No more chemicals can be used on this property for any purpose," she told them. "We can't protect you against ants, water bugs, termites, moths, salamanders or dragons?" they protested. "Goodbye. I'm sorry to lose you, but that's the way it is," was her reply.

A week later, the owner of the pest control company phoned my wife for an appointment. "Tell me, what are the products you are using that you told us were environmentally safe?" She showed him what she was using. The next month, the operator was back.

He asked us to go outside to see his familiar truck. Beneath his company name, painted in large letters, was an addition: "Organic Pest Control." He said, "I came to thank you. My business has never been better!"

In Santa Fe, we use a part-time housecleaner. She, too, received the directions "no more harmful chemicals." To replace them, my wife told her to use baking soda and vinegar for cleaning and non-phosphate soap in place of the standard washing machine products that get flushed into our waterways.

On our following trip to Santa Fe, the cleaner presented us with her new business card which read, "Suzie Smith—Organic Housecleaning." She reported that she had experienced a fifty percent increase in business once she had switched from chemicals dangerous to the environment (and that means to all of us) and had replaced them with simple products that cause no damage.

No owner of a business wants to have to change his traditional, most profitable product lines. The coal companies opposed regulation of the use of soft coals which produce toxic fumes; the automobile makers resisted legislation to force them to develop engines that spew less carbon monoxide into the air; the petrochemical industry is still fighting against regulations against plastics that are non-biodegradable.

At long last the Senate has passed a clean air bill with the half-hearted aid of the Bush administration. Factory and product changes are expensive, but so is the poisoning of the environment.

Business has to face up to the fact that environmental concern is here to stay. The public in every democratic country has made up its mind that it wants to live in a cleaner, safer world. Politicians and business leaders who ignore that mandate do so at their own risk.

Grandparents Fade from Picture

Not too long ago, children went to their grandparents' house for dinner every Sunday. Now, they are more likely to be taken to a fast food restaurant. Is a vital connection being broken? Is something precious being lost?

As part of the new social contract of the twentieth century, America has reduced the scope of the family and turned to television and institutions such as schools and day-care centers to take its place.

The current generation of grandparents has been the first to be set apart, and, in a sense, it is their own fault. Today's grandparents were proud of their children's achievements, but they raised their kids to be independent of Mom and Dad. Now, they turn around and discover that their children are no longer emotionally attached. They have moved away, geographically as well as psychologically.

In a recent study, 300 children, many too young to verbalize their feelings, were asked to draw pictures of their grandparents. The five percent or so who regularly saw their grandparents picture them as pleasantly larger than life, smack in the center of the paper, sometimes at the base of a family pyramid.

Many of the others drew their grandparents as relatively small figures at the left of the page, a telling sign that they were accustomed to saying goodbye or that the grandparents seemed to be passing out of their lives.

Many grandparents speak nostalgically of the places where they once spent relaxing hours with their own grandparents—the kitchen, the porch, the attic, the pantry—most of which are no longer to be found in modern homes.

These observations reflect on the most troublesome phenomenon of our time, namely, the breakup of the family, resulting in a state of familial anarchy that is the base cause of many of our problems related to crime, school dropouts, drug use and unemployment.

There is nothing new about this statement that has not been enunciated time and again by speakers, educators, ministers and teachers. The trouble is that we have not committed ourselves to solving the problem of how to put Humpty Dumpty together again.

Grandparents and grandchildren suffer equally from the gap of close relationships. As a general rule, they do not have to do anything to make each other happy. Their happiness comes from being together. Underestimating the importance of that kind of relationship is indeed a tragic loss. Perhaps a nation dedicated to putting families together would learn how to unscramble the eggs caused by Mr. Dumpty's fall off the wall.

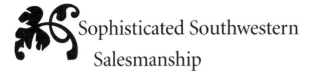Sophisticated Southwestern Salesmanship

Another Santa Fe Indian Market has come and gone, and I am once again impressed at how much the Pueblo Indians have learned about marketing since their East Coast brothers sold Manhattan Island for $24 to the Dutch gentry.

The day when the white man could exploit the Indian has long gone, especially when shopping for the fine Southwestern crafts that have become collectors' items. I am thinking particularly about blackware, the fine pottery that is the specialty of two neighboring pueblos near Santa Fe, New Mexico.

It looks as if it were carved from onyx or jet rather than shaped from ordinary red clay. It owes its lustrous, deep sheen not to glaze but to hours of painstaking polishing with smooth stones. The best of these potters can and do receive thousands of dollars for each pot. Yet they sell these valuable pieces from rough wooden booths in the carnival-like atmosphere of the Santa Fe market or the state fair in Albuquerque.

If collectors hope to buy a specific piece from one of the more celebrated potters, they must arise before dawn and line up, or they will arrive to find the stock is sold out. Fistfights over who gets which pot have been known to break out between potential customers.

The potters could easily and more comfortably sell all they can produce through galleries, or directly to the collectors who seek them out at their homes throughout the year, but they are as canny about publicity as any Seventh Avenue dress designer. They know that to have their buyers jockeying for position before dawn enhances the legend.

This event, which started sixty-eight years ago with an exhibition of Indian arts and crafts, has become one of the largest craft shows in the nation. The plaza in the center of Santa Fe is taken over by exhibitions, with booths erected over every square foot and now spilling over into adjacent side streets to accommodate the growing number of artisans who show their wares.

The Southwest Association on Indian Affairs, a permanent organization consisting of local citizens and Indians from the thirty tribes in the area, has formed to establish the rules for exhibition, and to bestow prizes to the artisans in the various categories of production. The attendance grows from year to year, reaching a peak of 80,000 in 1989. The Indians accept personal checks and credit cards. It is not unusual to see bank drafts from Connecticut, New York, Michigan, Ohio and California, as well as nearby Texas and Oklahoma.

Some may say the Indians are no longer being exploited but are the exploiters. As a former retailer, I take off my hat to the sophisticated merchandising of the artisans of the Southwest.

Name Alone Does Not Ensure High Quality

When we buy jewelry, the terms "14-karat" and "sterling" give us some assurance of standards of quality—or at least we think so.

Those terms can be deceptive, though, for while they describe the content of metal objects, they do not comment on the relative thickness or weight. A pin may be correctly labeled as 14-karat gold, but the metal may be paper thin and, consequently, a third of the price of the identical design made of a thicker piece of 14-karat gold. Obviously, the heavier piece will be less subject to dents and damage.

This point was brought home to me a number of years ago when the firm with which I was associated cataloged a sterling silver telephone dialer. Shortly after the ad appeared, I received a chiding note from my friend, Walter Hoving, then chairman of Tiffany and Company, who wrote, "Your company should be ashamed for selling such a poor piece of merchandise. Even though it can be labeled in truth as sterling, the metal is so thin it had to be filled with plaster to give it any weight."

When I showed our buyer the letter and the cut-through section of the dialer that Mr. Hoving had returned, she was defensive. "It's only $5.95," she said. "What more can you expect? Besides, we've received over a thousand orders."

"That makes it even worse," I replied. "Cancel the orders, withdraw the item from your stocks and never justify a poor piece of merchandise on the grounds of price."

From then on, we redoubled our efforts to check the weight of all articles made of precious or semiprecious metals. Mr. Hoving taught me an important lesson and I was grateful for the constructive criticism.

Unfortunately, other commodities we purchase have to be similarly analyzed. "Pure silk" may be so thin that the product made from it is shoddy, or it can be used to describe a magnificent textile.

"Pure wool" does not describe the origin of the wool, which determines to a great extent its value. Wool from the clip of a domestic sheep is not as valuable as that which comes off the back of an Australian or Tasmanian animal. Better yet, shahtoosh wool from the neck of the rare ibex goat, which inhabits the lofty Himalayas, costs $2.20 per square inch, making a man's muffler retail for more than $400 and a woman's shawl for about $2,500.

The lesson of all this is to avoid making valuations of anything until you learn all about it, and you can learn all about it with a little effort.

Take any commodity you choose and study it by going to three or four stores that carry the product in which you have an interest. Tell the salesperson. Explain to the people behind the counter what you are trying to accomplish and you will be surprised by how helpful they will be. Compare one quality next to the other, whether it be pearls or furs or silver. You will find that this method of study will teach you the differences in quality very quickly.

John Ruskin wrote, "Quality is never an accident. It's always the result of intelligent effort. It's the will to produce a superior thing."

1991

Murdering Ideas Should Be Criminal

All of us have had an idea that we thought was great and taken it to someone we respected, only to hear him or her reply, "Ah, it really doesn't grab me."

Have you ever stopped to think that it takes only one good idea to change any endeavor from failure to success? Most major corporations are built on the solid rock of one good idea or one sound business concept. Today, more than ever, we need the strength of fresh, new ideas, but ideas don't come in do-it-yourself kits or by the bottle. They are rarely fully assembled.

That means we have to guard against the ways in which we kill ideas. We need to make sure that each idea is given plenty of time and room to grow and mature. There are standard phrases that kill ideas; they are the poison darts that make them wilt and die. Here's one, for example: "Do you really think that will work?" Or how about this: "That's a great idea, but. . . . " And another: "You know, I had an idea like that a long time ago."

These are hasty judgments that usually serve no purpose other than showing that the person who says them does not want to be bothered. What is actually needed is a healthy dose of listening and understanding. New ideas can seem fantastic or impossible, judged by today's knowledge. Our horizons are constantly widening, and what seems out of the question today may very possibly be something you will want for Christmas next year.

Idea murdering is not against the law, unfortunately, and unless an individual has great tenacity, good ideas may be slaughtered, not just by enemies, but by friends as well. It is so easy to stifle a fresh idea on the grounds that it's not new or that it was tried before and failed. Even if the idea is not new, each period of time is new, and under new conditions, even a failed idea of the past might succeed today.

No one has a monopoly on idea creativity, and no one has the judgment of a Solomon in determining the worth of new concepts. These are precepts that all of us who are called upon to appraise new ideas should keep in mind.

From my days as a retailer, I recall a buyer who stifled any fresh idea offered by a subordinate with, "We tried that eight years ago, and it didn't work," or, "We advertised similar raincoats back when I first started, and they laid an egg." She had a long, partial memory, but she forgot that the raincoat that didn't sell was advertised in the midst of a ten-month drought.

Mark Twain was known to have invested heavily in many inventions, but one inventor went away from Mr. Twain's house empty-handed. That inventor was Alexander Graham Bell. The invention Mr. Twain turned down was the telephone. He didn't think it would work.

Learning a Lesson with Jade

In detective stories, the important clues are those that concern motive and opportunity. The clues about method are just thrown in to keep the reader off the track. There may be a similar confusion in our school system.

At least two generations of children have grown up while educators are debating why Johnny can't read. Most often, it's the same old argument over phonetics vs. the "look and say" method. Both sides overlook the fact that some children learn and some fail with either technique and neither asks why.

I am reminded of the old story about a Chinese elder who lost $10,000 on a deal that involved fake jade. A purported expert offered, for another $10,000, to teach him about jade. He accepted eagerly and arrived promptly for his first lesson, but he found no one there. He did discover, however, a note from his teacher, anchored to a table with a piece of jade. It said the teacher was detained and that he should wait.

After an hour, the businessman left. This pattern was repeated for several weeks. Although the teacher promised to return soon, the businessman was left alone with nothing but the note held down by a piece of jade. While he was waiting, he read the only book in the room, a textbook on jade, from which he learned the characteristics of real and fake jade. Finally, a week later, instead of the usual note under the jade, there was the teacher's bill for $10,000. The businessman was enraged. "I've been cheated again," he said. "After neglecting me for weeks, my so-called teacher has the nerve to present me with a bill. And, to add insult to injury, he's left his bill underneath a piece of false jade!"

The moral, of course, is that faced with boredom, the business-man was motivated to teach himself by reading a book.

In my own educational experience, I encountered two basic types of teachers. First, there were the teachers who knew their subjects and raced the students through the syllabus, completing it just as the term ended. Then, there were other teachers who spent half the course time stimulating students to do extra reading that helped them understand the subjects in depth. Invariably, at term's end, they had completed only one half of the syllabus.

The latter are the teachers I remember most fondly, for they taught me the value and rewards of curiosity, a quality closely related to research.

I have never seen a preschooler who was not eager to learn. The motive is already there. It remains the task of the educators to concentrate less on method and more on providing the oppor-tunity.

Travel Can Make Us Think

Travel advertisements abound with lean, perfectly tanned couples cavorting in beautiful surf, but I have noticed a different approach to travel promotion by two popular vacation destinations—Jamaica and New Mexico.

What do we really want in a vacation? A change of scenery? Romance? A taste of the exotic? Probably all of these things, in varying degrees depending on our own station in life at the moment. These are the things the travel posters typically promise us. Implicit in all travel, and so taken for granted we don't think about it, is the lure of the difference in people.

Jamaica and New Mexico come right out and say it in their travel campaigns: Come see our people. Their posters show faces—black faces, brown faces, red faces—different faces. My first reaction to this kind of advertising was negative. As a sometime-resident of New Mexico, I did not want the people I had come to know as friends and neighbors gawked at like animals in a zoo. Then I realized that the curiosity we exhibit toward a different culture is really curiosity about ourselves.

We wonder, "What would I be like if I had been born in another time, another race, another place?" So we buy and wear the local clothing, eat the local food and learn the local history in order to "try on," for the length of the vacation, a different personality. But the big difference is people, so our most memorable vacations turn out to be those when we were fortunate to make friends with some of the "natives," whether they were Neapolitan, Nepalese or North Carolinian.

The beginning of knowledge comes, it seems to me, when we encounter different folkways, different ways of using a dinner knife and fork, different ways of cooking the things we eat for dinner, different ways of expressing politeness and enthusiasm, different values of what is considered fair play.

When we took our children to Europe on their first trip back in the late forties, we told them that we didn't care what they saw or learned, but we wanted them to observe how many things the Europeans did differently than we did then, whether it be the manner in which the French set the dining table, or the way the Belgians stacked hay, or the differences between a German and a British breakfast. They entered the spirit of my challenge and took great delight in pointing out their discoveries. They lost any sense of smugness they might have possessed, and I am happy to say they have never gotten it back.

When we know a person from a different culture, we find we are more alike than not. Such a revelation destroys romantic illusion but makes our peaceful sharing of this tiny planet more plausible.

Bargains Do Not Mean Lack of Style

In these days of rising prices, it is very difficult for people to maintain any established standard of living.

In America, unlike Europe, retail merchants clear their stocks seasonally. That is why you see such sharp reductions in January and July when stores are marking merchandise down thirty percent to sixty percent from the original prices. These reductions do not indicate that the merchandise is not good. They simply mean that the merchant has accumulated a lot of broken styles, sizes and colors that become difficult to sell.

As new merchandise arrives, a merchant is faced with the dilemma of either finding a place for his carry-overs, or clearing them out at great reductions. It may seem costly, but in the long run, retailers find that it is more profitable to maintain new and current stocks than to fall in love with the jewels of a previous season and keep them on the shelves.

Thus astute shoppers can go into any of the good stores in the country at clearance time and buy clothes at a fraction of what they would have to pay at the outset of the season. Back in the thirties, we used to call such customers "bargain hunters." The only way they could dress as well as they desired was to take advantage of the bargains. They waited for the clearances; they still do today.

One of my friends falls in this category, and she dresses very well, indeed, due to her everwatchfulness and her good, selective eye. This year, she found a Yves St. Laurent suit for fifty percent off, and a wonderful ski outfit in a last-call sale at seventy percent off the original price, enabling her to be a smash hit on the Colorado slopes this winter. She bought a marvelous leather jacket made in Spain at less than half its original price. True, there wasn't much from which to select; there was only one jacket left in her size and in a desirable color, but one was all she wanted. She sacrificed selection in order to take advantage of a bargain.

She went to a gift store clearance and purchased four wedding gifts of top quality at thirty-five percent of the original price, making it possible to send finer presents than she could have afforded at regular prices. She does not buy at sale time only, but she maintains a sharp watch throughout the year for occasional close-out opportunities. Stores need buyers for their markdowns as much as they need them for regular-priced purchases. Actually, the only way a store can maintain large assortments of regular-priced merchandise is by having a market for articles that are reduced.

Anyone buying from the sales rack is deserving of as much attention and assistance as those paying full price. Store owners recognize this. Unfortunately, some members of their sales staff have not learned this important fact of life. Curiously, though, few store operations display their sales goods with any style or flair, nor do they remind their staffs each day of the sale: "Be nice to your sales customers; they are important to us."

This is a sure way to beat the HCL ("high cost of living," as we used to call it) and to maintain the quality standards to which we have become accustomed.

Do Not Let Your Dreams Die Easily

If you have ever wanted to play the piano but hesitated because you are no Van Cliburn, remember the motto of Harry Belten, a character in a short story written by Barry Targan: "If a thing is worth doing, it is worth doing badly."

In the short story, Belten was an average, hard-working hardware salesman whose hobby was the violin. He had supported his family, put two kids through college and almost had the mortgage paid. Then, at age fifty-one, he began to act strangely. He took a second mortgage on the house and used the money to hire an orchestra and a concert hall so that he could perform the solo part of the Mendelssohn Violin Concerto.

Now, even though Harry had taken lessons since 1941 as a violinist, he was a good hardware salesman. His family thought he was crazy and urged him to see a psychiatrist. Harry did not want to upset anybody; all he wanted was to play the concerto with a real orchestra in front of a real audience, but to make his wife and kids happy, he went to the psychiatrist and explained.

The doctor listened and then told Harry that his ambition was merely his way of striking back at the subconscious frustrations of his small, unexciting life. After a few sessions together, he and the doctor could probably overcome Harry's compulsion to give the concert. Harry agreed with the analysis but asked why the solution might not be for him to go ahead with the thrill and excitement of the concert. The doctor said, "Why not? If you can afford it, try it."
It is too bad that we have become a nation of spectators because we have not learned, with Harry Belten, that you do not have to be perfect to experience the thrill of achievement.

At the time of my eightieth birthday, friends asked what I had not done in my life that I had always wanted to do. In jest, I replied, "I've always wanted to be a clown in a circus." When my birthday came a few months later, I was presented with a four-color billboard announcing the appearance of Stanley Marcus as ringmaster for a day in the Ringling Brothers and Barnum and Bailey Circus at Madison Square Garden in New York City.

I picked a Sunday in May for my debut at the circus and was assigned to the chief clown, who was to be my tutor. In a few hours he instructed me in the fundamentals of clownsmanship and then urged me to take a half-hour nap before the performance.

Promptly at 1 P.M., I went through makeup and costuming to prepare me for the grand opening parade at 2 P.M. I circled the arena with my fellow clowns, imitating what they were doing and improvising on my own. It wasn't difficult at all.

For the evening performance I donned my full dress suit and silk topper. I used the whistle with which I was supplied, stepped forth into the center ring to the microphone, and before 18,000 spectators, announced, "Ladeez and gentlemen. Welcome to the greatest show on Earth, the Ringling Brothers and Barnum & Bailey Circus!"

I, unlike Harry Belten, was able to do what I had yearned to do without visiting a psychiatrist.

Why Be a Walking Billboard?

The practice of imprinting, embroidering or weaving the name of the fashion designer into an article of apparel started in the mid-1950s, when a woman named Countess Mara decided to market a line of men's neckties on the front of which she had embroidered her initials, C.M., beneath her noble crown. She came to me seeking both my advice and an order. As an experienced merchant, I gave her the former but not the latter.

I told her that American men would not buy her ties on three counts. First, they would resent the fact that a woman was presuming to design for men. Second, they would object to the use of the crown as a symbol of royalty. And finally, her designs, which were bold and flamboyant, ran counter to the prevailing fashion trend for small, neat, geometric patterns.

She did not follow my counsel but proceeded to market her product, which met with resounding success. This experience has made me very humble about giving fashion advice to anyone with a new idea.

Shortly after that, a young impoverished nobleman in Florence, Italy, the Marchese de Pucci, embarked on a fashion career by designing bold fabrics which he made into scarves, blouses and dresses. He incorporated his signature very inconspicuously into the pattern of his printed designs.

As a result of previous experience, I had learned a lesson, so I made no effort to dissuade him from using his name. His clothes, in brilliant colors, were immediately snapped up by a public that was tired of the drabness of wartime apparel.

His success was quickly noted by other European and American designers, who signed or initialed almost every product they made. Many customers, unsure of their own tastes, decided that if the name of a great designer was on the garment, it must, therefore, be in the height of fashion.

Will customers continue to be willing to be walking, unpaid billboards for fashion creators? In some cases, designers bribe retailers to publicize their products by providing advertising dollars, personal appearances or exclusivities. Most retailers fall for these inducements and end up providing a launching platform for unknown designers.

In fashion, the pendulum swings both ways, and many discriminating customers are rebelling now against the Vs and Gs that adorn their neckties, handbags and blouses. If they want an initial or signature, they want their own. The only valid label on a product is that of the manufacturer or seller who guarantees satisfaction or money back, an assurance that designers do not normally provide.

Penny Pinching Can Be Costly

A newsletter from a Wall Street adviser came to my desk; it was headed by an anonymous quotation that read, "Nothing recedes like excess." He should know. During boom times, it is a rare business that does not build up its expenses beyond prudent limits.

It is common knowledge that a recession is the free enterprise system's way of exerting self-discipline, of getting the force of supply and demand into relative balance, of curtailing the excesses and extravagances encouraged by years of prosperity during which we humans, for the most part, forget all of the lessons of prudence.

To survive the economic crunch, business as well as individuals are forced to retrench and to reduce expenditures to meet diminished income. It is not a very pleasant undertaking; spending is much more fun.

Trade journals are filled with tips for cost reductions, ranging from cutting pencils in half to curtailing the number of rank-and-file staff members. Rarely, however, does one read an article on "How to reduce brass to make silver dollars." Corporate headquarters is usually the last spot that feels the effects of a recession.

Penny-pinching techniques that save thousands of pennies also damage customer service and loyalties. On a recent two-hour mid-morning airline flight, economies were very evident. Facial tissue had been eliminated from the lavatories, and food service had been reduced from snack to small bun.

That probably saved forty-two cents per passenger; and multiplied by the number of flights a day, it probably achieved a considerable economy. The manner of delivery of this lonesome bun, minus butter or jam, was a different matter. The flight attendant presented it on a small paper napkin with an apologetic manner. Estimated savings over a small paper plate: a half-cent. That's penny-pinching.

The explanation she gave, that this was part of the cost-savings program, embarrassed even an employee of fifteen years' airline service. It was that kind of economy that will not be forgotten, particularly since the price of the ticket was $583 first class, from Dallas to Colorado Springs.

Peter Tischman, the managing director of the newly restored St. Regis Hotel, said in a *New York Times* interview, "The recession has wounded even some of New York's finest hotels." He went on to say, "There is always room at the top, regardless of what happens."

Hotels, restaurants, stores and everyone in the customer service business face the same needs to reduce costs. So far, they have done a better job than the major airlines; they do not annoy their customers by miserly economies. Pinch dollars, not pennies!

If It's Worth Doing, Do It Urgently

Years ago, a European refugee taught me a very valuable lesson. He was a Czechoslovakian who had been in the textile business in Prague. He came to the United States during World War II and started a fabric importing business.

He brought to this country certain cloths that had been developed in Great Britain to his very exacting standards. His gabardines were the most luxurious, his worsteds were the crispest; both were the most expensive we had ever seen but worth the price to anyone seeking the best.

I have met many good and great salesmen in my life, but never had I seen a seller who showed his wares with such vigor, or extolled his products with such enthusiasm, or sold with such a sense of urgency. He approached every sale as if it were the last one he would ever make. His spirit was infectious; and before he was through with his presentation, I wanted to buy as if it were the last chance I would ever have to purchase such fine cloth.

In a mere two years he built the best luxury fabric business in the country. After one buying session, I turned to him and said, "You approach business with such a great sense of urgency, I wonder if you brush your teeth with that same spirit?"

"Why, of course," he replied. "I do brush my teeth urgently, as I do anything in life that's worth doing at all."

Whether he knew it or not, he was a disciple of the noted eighteenth-century German philosopher Georg Hegel, who declared, "Nothing has been accomplished without passion. The whole will and character must be devoted to accomplish one aim."

If we reflect on the great achievers from Alexander the Great to Thomas Edison, from Louis Pasteur to Jack Nicklaus, it is probable that they all shared in that common trait.

Life is too short to defer actions until tomorrow, life is too challenging with potential accomplishments to waste precious time by putting things off.

Great salesmen—be they purveyors of jewels, automobiles or paintings—have a common characteristic; they present their works with vigor, which produces an enthusiasm that communicates the excitement of the seller to the buyer. They never have to mention the word urgency; it is transmitted by voice and manner.

As a result of my experience with my Czechoslovakian friend, I amended my grandmother's advice of "Anything worth doing is worth doing well" to "Anything worth doing is worth doing urgently."

1992

Be Prepared to Look Foolish

A friend who produces a newsletter for his employees favors me with copies, and, more times than not, I feel their arrival has the physical effect not unlike the prick of a pin—just enough to startle me but not deep enough to draw blood.

His notes are always printed on a vertically lined note paper. The type naturally crosses the lines instead of following them.

Being struck by the fact that most of the people in his office type on the lines instead of across them caused the writer to challenge the lack of venturesomeness in his associates. Since his business deals with creativity of ideas, it was natural for him to notice that no one dared to write across the lines. Why not? he queried.

This led to a message from him on the barriers to creativity. How many of these come about as a result of education, or as part of the surrounding organization structure, or a desire not to rock the boat?

Creativity, in its best sense, relates to doing something in a new way. It may even be reclaiming something old and doing it anew from a fresh vantage point. It may be a bold jump into an uncharted path that reveals no obvious ending.

My friend, who has great confidence in the funds of creativeness in the intellectual bank of his associates, issues a very simple rule for creativity, "Be prepared to look foolish." He goes on to say, "If you are unwilling to risk derision from those whose conventional wisdom is threatened by your idea, or if you are overly bothered by the snickers of those who take comfort in the 'tried and true,' it's unlikely you'll be very creative."

Our current economic recession calls for solutions that are bold and innovative. It hungers for those who are prepared to look foolish as they propose new ideas and concepts. Every business in our free-enterprise system is holding its breath until some member of its staff comes forth with a new technique for either manufacturing or selling an old product, or with a new idea for something that is both needed and wanted. Our economic recovery needs an infusion of newness, appropriate for our times, as badly as it needs fresh political voices.

It is not a new technique for the president of company to bang on the table and say, "You've got to sell more." That strategy hasn't worked since the wagon makers in the early twentieth century tried to discourage the sale of automobiles by calling on the salesmen to block the demand for "these new fangled machines that will scare the cows and the babies."

As an ex-retailer, I never had success in selling two left shoes to my customers any more than American automobile dealers are finding in trying to sell our left-hand drive cars to the Japanese, who drive on the left side of the road.

 The Myth of Shopping

The sources of myths are clothed in anonymity. No one knows exactly who originated them or even where they started. Some are centuries old; some have a vintage date of only a dozen years. Some may have validity; others are out of date but unburied.

One of the most common myths believed by many retailers is that customers enjoy shopping. I suspect this idea gained credence in the early part of the century when women had a great deal more leisure than they do today and when stores were filled with a constant flow of new wonders. Ready-to-wear was a fresh concept at that time, and customers were agog at the wide assortment of goods ranging from dresses off the rack to ready-made hats.

Upper- and middle-class women were not involved in PTAs, symphony leagues, charity balls, committees or continuing education. So what was better entertainment for an afternoon than going to town with the girls and seeing the latest fashion arrivals?

Today, women are either working or are committed to a wide variety of activities that consume their spare time. Transportation is faster but more difficult, stores have been forced to set up security precautions to protect their stocks from shoplifters, many salespeople tend to be less interested in customers' needs than in their own social activities, and, finally, merchandise offerings in general are repetitious between stores and consequently less exciting.

There are many retailers who still believe that their customers like to shop. I suspect they have talked without listening. As far as I'm concerned, this is a myth whose time has come to be interred.

Formerly, department stores had wider ranges of departments, such as furniture stores and refrigerators, book departments, toys, electronics and bridal shops, many of which have been eliminated because of space requirements or mark-up limitations.

The tendency of many retailers, specialty stores included, has been to replace marginal profit producers specialized apparel operations that can be counted on for greater profitability per square foot.

This is a perfectly rational approach, but this solution ignores a resulting side effect. As stores become more and more packed with ready-to-wear departments, they may become more profitable for the moment, but they also become less interesting to the customer.

When stores become less exciting because of sterility of the merchandise mix, there is a strong likelihood that boredom will set in. Coupled with the decline in exclusive merchandise lines, the stocks of competitive stores begin to mirror each other. Stores are buying the same merchandise from the same manufacturers in the same colors and in the same "packages" dictated by the sellers. Individualized selections by creative buyers have been curtailed and restricted by the requirements of mass distribution.

This danger of boredom I don't think is an exaggeration. In a society in which impulse buying is an important factor, then the excitement created by new and beautiful merchandise becomes an important factor in drawing buyers to the marketplace.

Sometime ago in a speech, I commented that I was fully expectant of a newspaper headline that would appear someday that would read, "Prominent socialite found dead in shopping center. Authorities claim she was bored to death."

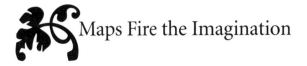

Maps Fire the Imagination

Maps, whether they are in a world atlas or in Mapsco, are tremendously useful inventions to help us find our way in new territory. But while I have always used maps when traveling, I enjoy them more when they show me not where I am going but where I have been.

Among the many delightful things in this world, none ignites my imagination more than maps. I can pore over any map for hours. It makes little difference whether it's of a place I know well or a place I will never see.

Maps are like time capsules that show us not only the geography of a place but the philosophy of a time. The older a map is, the better I like it. Just a few years before Columbus brought another hemisphere to the attention of the Western world, old maps showed sea monsters guarding the huge chasm where medieval man thought the world ended somewhere a few miles west of Scotland. Old maps documented man's hopes as well as his fears. Incidentally, the Cartographic History Library at the University of Texas in Arlington is the best in this part of the country and was the source of the Admiral's Map reproduced in the Somesuch Press's *Tabula Terra Nova*, produced to celebrate the quincentennial of Columbus's voyage to America.

Once the New World was discovered, it took explorers years to resign themselves to the fact that there was no easy way to cross our vast continent. This belief in the existence of a Northwest Passage was so strong that many early cartographers drew one in, extending the St. Lawrence River across the Grand Canyon to connect with the Pacific around Mount St. Helen's.

Then there were the maps in my grammar school geography. Vast stretches surrounding either pole were marked "unexplored," fueling my imagination with Northwest Passages and monsters of my own with the flood of new knowledge. Today, school books have accurate maps of the topography of Jupiter's moons and the moon's valleys as well.

Nowadays, every foot of our planet has been mapped, and we chart the very heavens. A future generation may find our star maps, populated with black holes, as charmingly naive as we do our ancestors' sea monsters. There is still a lot about the world we need to know.

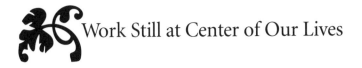# Work Still at Center of Our Lives

When the Garden of Eden was foreclosed, Adam and Eve had to go to work. Work has never recovered from that humiliation. From the very beginning, work has been something bad—a punishment. Only money makes it desirable.

From the time we are old enough to know the difference, our lamentations fill the air about how awful work is. And, in response, management wails that nobody wants to work anymore! American productivity—once a standard for the world—has dipped to an embarrassingly uncompetitive low.

And yet, for generations of Americans, work was rewarding. The humbling toil of an illiterate grandfather got the son a foothold and a high school education. The dogged persistence of the son saw the grandson through college or even law school. The motive of work was everything.

To work for mere survival is desperate; to work for a better life for one's children and grandchildren lends a dignity to one's labor. That dignity is the quality that many of us find missing today. Americans prone to restlessness about the spiritual disappointments of work should consult the unemployed men and women in our own midst. They know all about the personal dignity that a job brings.

Work is still the complicated and crucial center of most lives. We are what we do, simply because that is where we spend most of our waking hours. And, like it or not, while mobility weakens our family ties, our co-workers often form our new family—our tribe —our social world.

A newly elected administration's major platform is the recognition of the need to put people back to work. It won't be easy, as President-elect Bill Clinton knew when he repeated the pledge of creating jobs during his zigzagging campaign across America. He knew it would be bad, but he knew that this was America's single greatest need.

Health protection and rights of personal choice were also important issues, but they cannot be solved without the restoration of an economy that encourages employment. Franklin Roosevelt was faced with this same problem but in a greater degree. He entertained and experimented with a variety of ideas on how to accomplish employment. He spent hundreds of millions of dollars in his efforts to create work, for which he was rewarded by a large body of votes.

Wishful thinking and devout prayers will not create a single job. Only a program of vast size and innovation will get the world on the move again. The money this will take needs to be paid today and not charged to our children.

Perils of Return to Small Towns

The social scientist tell us that we are in the midst of a migration from large cities to small towns. If you wonder whether or not you would like to make the change, I have developed a checklist to measure your rural compatibility.

From my experience with living in Santa Fe and my familiarity with the nearby villages, I know there is a degree of culture shock for those accustomed to the sophistication and convenience of big city life. So before you decide to make the move to a more pastoral life, you should consider these things:

Do you like the idea of answering a wrong number but recognizing the caller's voice anyway? Do you mind giving strangers directions not by street number, but by landmarks? How do you feel about a social life where the number of theaters and discos can be counted on one hand and the community's big event is the arrival of the mail at the post office?

Do you find it appealing to be so familiar with the mayor and the sheriff that you know what they like for breakfast and what their kids made on their college entrance exams? Do you mind that they know the same things about you?

Can you stand the inconvenience of a limited selection of merchandise in the local store, and are you patient enough to wait while your needs are being special ordered? Will you understand when the local news sources give you more information on the latest controversy over dog licensing than on the situation in Russia? Do you mind being the last person in the entire country to know that there is a shortage of tablecloths in the White House?

Obviously, there are advantages to the country life, but it appears to me that civilization started to advance in the middle ages when people moved into the cities for a variety of reasons. The city provided protection against the roving bands of barbarians (and that is something that our cities must do better than they have been doing). Cities provide entertainment that is not feasible in small towns; cities provide a variety of experiences ranging from good adventures to sports events, and exposure to ballet and musical productions made possible by population concentrations.

Obviously, electronic communications have helped even the score immensely, but until we have "smell-a-vision" and "touch-a-vision" we are getting only a small share of personal dividend from just watching or listening to the reports of what is happening.

If any of these items on my list raises doubts in your mind, then maybe you had better use the time you're caught in a traffic jam on the freeway to count the blessings of city life.

1993

We Should Encourage the Dreamers

In *The New York Times* obituary article on Steve Ross, the writer quoted the advice given Mr. Ross some years ago by his dying father. His sole inheritance from his father, he said, consisted of this admonition: "There are those who work all day; those who dream all day; and those who spend an hour dreaming before setting to work to fulfill those dreams."

"Go into the third category," his father said, "because there's virtually no competition."

These words made a deep impact on the teenager, as he was fond of telling his friends in later years.

We are all familiar with the traditional counsel given to young people about working hard and being frugal, but parents, grandfathers and uncles usually emphasize industriousness, with few encouraging words for the dreamers.

The latter is left for the poets who, over the centuries, have established themselves as the self-appointed patron saints for those who contemplate and dream. The annals of history are filled, of course, with the memories of the legions who had neither the desire nor ability to put their dreams into action. Those rare individuals who could do both are the ones who make history, and there are many whose accomplished dreams are evidenced in Dallas today. The Texas Instruments founders—Eugene McDermott, J. Erik Jonsson and Cecil Green—are in the forefront of our memories, as are the recollections of such names as Karl Hoblitzelle, Fred Florence and R. L. Thornton.

My father, Herbert Marcus, the co-founder of Neiman Marcus,

was one of those who did both. He was actually labeled "the dreamer" by his business and social associates in the early years of this century, when at the age of twenty, he expounded at length on his ambitions and how he was going to accomplish them.

Few took him seriously, writing him off as another of those impractical young guys who had his head in the sky. After he started to work for Sanger Bros. as a buyer of boys' clothing, his supervisors recognized that while he did a lot of dreaming, he also worked all day, and worked hard at that.

His dreams were well expressed eighty-five years ago, when Neiman Marcus opened its doors. The initial advertisement in *The Dallas Morning News*, September 10, 1907, which he wrote personally because he could not afford an advertising manager, spelled out his dreams for a new type of store for the Southwest.

Throughout his life, he never ceased to dream an hour before setting to work to fulfill his dreams. Best of all, he conveyed his dreams to all who were associated with him. He never wavered, when the chips were down, in defending his dreams.

In all fields of endeavor, women and men have dreamed of new solutions, new ideas. The past has never satisfied them, for they have been able to envision fresh solutions just over the horizon.

We've had many such dreamers in Dallas and Texas and our country. To those who have worked all day and have devoted an hour a day to dreaming, we are deeply indebted.

Dallas is in need today of more of those who follow the advice of the senior Mr. Ross.

Disarmament Should Begin at Home

President Clinton was recently quoted as being disturbed and disappointed by North Korea's pullout from the Nuclear Non-proliferation Treaty, an international agreement that limits the spread of nuclear weapons.

If that incident is not enough to worry the world, look at the murky picture of the dispersed control of nuclear warheads among several of the dissident states in Russia.

So much for disarmament attempts on a global scale. Why should we expect the world to be willing to disarm when we Americans fail to agree among ourselves that the indiscriminate sale of handguns is an acceptable practice?

We want to disarm the world, but we refuse to disarm ourselves. We want to ban nuclear bombs in North Korea, but we do not want to give up the right to buy semi-automatic weapons in Texas and most other states.

An observer from Mars might characterize this apparent paradox as a demonstration of national hypocrisy.

On the same day that *The Dallas Morning News* carried an account of the president's reaction to the North Korean pullout, there was a front-page story about the death of an eighth-grade student in a West Dallas school.

This well-written story commented, "Only one subject was taught Monday in the eighth-grade classroom at the St. Mary of Carmel Catholic School: death."

Students prayed and wrote letters to their slain classmate, Edith Medina. One letter by Esther Ornelas, thirteen, stated: "Every time

I look at the sky, I see a shiny star and say, 'That's you.' It's better living up in heaven than in today's world"—a sad and poignant commentary from one so young.

The death of this innocent child, caused by shots from a passing car, was without provocation. The article went on to note that "police are baffled by the shooting and have no suspects in the case."

Our visitor from Mars would be quick to observe that there was no evidence of a public outcry, or a mass protest against a society that permits the access of weapons to any and all members of the population, including those who have a legitimate need to carry firearms as well as those who have no reason to possess them.

He would have to conclude that this is a very sick society in which such happenings occur somewhere, on a daily basis, in these United States, and more frequently in Texas than we care to admit.

Where are the indignant, concerned citizens, the business, religious and educational leaders? Have their voices been stilled by the gun interests, whose political action committees contribute to the financing of so many national and state elected officials?

Keeping the Brass Polished

During my active days as a retailer, I made it a practice to hold monthly meetings with the entire sales organization. I addressed the staff so many times on the subjects of service, attitudes and responsibilities that I became concerned that I had said everything that needed to be said. I presume preachers share the same experience of feeling they are constantly repeating themselves.

However, there are certain verities of both life in general, and of retailing, specifically, which require perpetual reiteration. I have always been concerned with the untapped capacities of human beings who only occasionally live up to their own potential. It has always bothered me when I know people with tremendous capabilities that are wasted because of a failure to use them.

One of the most popular of my lectures on this subject dealt with a comparison of human beings to brass. I cited a visit to the bridge of a naval vessel where the brass fittings gleamed like gold. I asked the captain how often they had to shine the brass. He replied, "Every day. From the minute you stop polishing it, it starts to tarnish, and as beautiful as brass looks when it is glowing, conversely it looks dirty and repulsive when it is dull."

I correlated this description to human beings, saying, "None of us is made of gold, we are made of brass. But we can look like gold if we work as hard polishing ourselves as a sailor does polishing the brass on a ship. It is nothing we can do once a week; it is consistent, daily effort that makes both the brass and our own performances shine. We can all rise to greater heights if we are willing to make the extra effort."

Looking good, as good as we are capable of looking, contributes to success. Employers naturally gravitate to bright-looking women and men; those with whom we work daily enjoy associating with those who look bright, just as the ship with shining brass is a happier one than another whose metal is dull and tarnished.

Scores of times I have been impressed by all levels of people in management, and in the work force, simply because they appear to be bright and shining. Those who are engaged in shining invariably have shining eyes, a sense of alertness and a quality of responsiveness; working with them is more fun than those with dull and negative qualities.

That advice may sound very trite, but it must have made an impression on many hundreds of people, for almost every week, even today, some former associate comes up to me and says, "I am still polishing my brass!"

French Set a Good Example

A few weeks ago on a pleasure trip to the South of France, I stumbled on a stairway as I was leaving a restaurant, and hit my head on one of the stone steps. My scalp was bleeding profusely; I felt stunned but otherwise evidenced no pain or discomfort.

The attendants immediately summoned an ambulance, which arrived quickly. The paramedics, who spoke some English, took my blood pressure and assured me that the doctor was on the way.

A few moments later, a small car arrived with an intern, who also spoke English. She examined me for the usual symptoms of a concussion. Finding none, she ordered the paramedics to put me in the ambulance, while she relayed her diagnosis to the hospital and advised that I was on the way.

Fifteen minutes later, without sirens, I arrived at the municipal hospital in the medieval city of Avignon. In a few minutes the surgeon arrived and, after looking at my wound, concurred with the intern that my injury was a lacerated scalp that required stitching.

On my entry into the hospital, no receiving desk clerk made inquiry about my life history, my antecedents, my permanent domicile or even my name. No questions were asked as to why I was in France, where I was staying or how I would pay for the emergency and ambulance services. The doctor did ask for my passport, which was returned to me a few minutes later. He took five stitches, gave me a tetanus shot, applied a bandage to my scraped right knee, took four X-rays and dismissed me.

When I asked for the bill, I was politely advised that it would be mailed to me in Dallas. The experience was unusual because of the complete absence of red tape that patients always encounter in trying to gain admission to a U.S. hospital.

Ten days later, my bill arrived. It was for a total of $213.32. I can only presume that the French medical system must have subsidized my care. However it was financed, the staff did a tremendously efficient job, without knowing whether or not the hospital would be paid. They trusted a complete, unidentified stranger.

Curiously enough, on my return home a week later, I read a column that appeared on the op-ed page of *The New York Times*, written by an American college professor, who had to undergo an emergency operation in the French city of Tours. His treatment was more serious than mine, as he had forty stitches to my five, but the attention he received and the absence of the American-style inquisition at the admission desk was identical with mine.

Vive la France!

Do Not Underrate Luck

You have doubtlessly heard the story about how a soldier's breast-pocket Bible stopped a bullet en route to his heart. Well, Bible or no Bible, luck had a lot to do with the eventual outcome.

Generally, luck is something that happens to individuals, although whole societies should not mock luck either. The Mayan civilization disappeared so strangely and suddenly that some massive stroke of bad luck may have been at work. The same might be said of another culture, such as that which built the stone pueblos at Chaco Canyon, New Mexico.

Of all civilizations, America has seemed the luckiest, with its vast spaces and natural resources. America became the place where the world came to get lucky. We had a whole western section of the country, which absorbed displaced families during times of recession, until it ran out of free space in the mid-twentieth century.

Luck is a strange, unknowable force that deposited Lana Turner in Schwab's Drug Store on Sunset Strip, that placed a football in Franco Harris's hands at the end of the Pittsburgh-Oakland championship in 1972, that prompted the Skylab to scatter its debris over western Australia instead of rush-hour Manhattan.

We have adopted two strategies toward luck. We woo and conjure it, hoping it will shower fortune on some lucky head. We dance, chant and study omens in an effort to ward off its more malicious and malevolent side.

Even so, one must have talent for luck, an ability to recognize an opportunity and run with it. It is true that people make their own luck, and good luck must have room to occur. Even though its mechanics remain perverse and mysterious, it can be encouraged and exploited.

Certain jewels are considered lucky and some, like opals, have a tradition of bad luck; some colors are considered lucky; $2 bills were regarded as unlucky, resulting in their eventual withdrawal from circulation; wearing a hat inside or raising an umbrella indoors is considered to be unlucky.

Bridal law decrees that a bride should wear "something borrowed, something blue, something old and something new," all in the name of luring the smiles of Lady Luck!

Baseball players and golfers observe so many rituals that they are convinced will affect the luck of performance, it would require a book to record them all.

It is fair to conclude, though, that good luck is more likely to occur to an individual who is positioned at the right place at the right time, trying to do something, rather than to the person who is just loafing.

Perhaps one purpose of luck, besides being a vast source of entertainment and conversation, is to illustrate to us all our common vulnerability—to make us more charitable toward one another. Well, maybe—if we're lucky!

Experience Is Not Wisdom

The combination of being an octogenarian and a professional consultant predisposes one to offer counsel and advice—even when it is not solicited. This is a tendency that requires a self-disciplined restraint.

Longevity does provide a lot of experience, but not necessarily with equal amounts of wisdom; at best, it furnishes perspective on issues and problems that may have come around a fourth and fifth time in the course of a lifetime.

Having seen how the same, or similar, circumstance worked out previously is helpful in assessing strategies, solutions and opportunities for those facing their first need for quick decisions. That, I guess, is what is meant by learning from experience.

The joke, of course, is that the same situations under exactly the same conditions rarely reappear. There is always a slight variant that denies the validity of a snap answer.

That is why I regard requests for advice—either paid or free—with a certain degree of concern. Solicitors for advice want the comfort of answers, whereas I feel more certain that I am better able to provide the right questions than the right answers. Giving positive answers is somewhat like passing spurious currency. The latter is against the law, but there is no punishment pertaining to sure-fire answers.

Some principles in business and daily life I hold to be true, such as integrity, the privileges guaranteed by the Bill of Rights, the Golden Rule, generosity of spirit, courtesy, fair play, intellectual honesty, the preciousness of time. There are others that I also practice, but with less intensity and conviction.

Many who seek advice are going through the motions of doing something they think they should do. Actually, they do not want advice; they simply want corroboration by another party that they are on the right course. Others have not thought out their problems and are searching for intellectual discipline. A minority have valid problems that benefit from intensive study and analysis with another person.

Newcomers to business often want to find success without paying the price of apprenticeship; they fail to understand that capital accumulation is the second step toward success, and that the first is to learn whatever they are attempting by working for someone else.

The greatest neophytes, of course, are those entering the frightening and rewarding area of matrimony. For them I pass on the only two rules for a happy marriage that I have learned from personal experience: first, never go to sleep on an unsolved disagreement with a spouse; and second, develop a short memory. No marital relationship is enhanced by remembering too much, too long. Minor grievances tend to become amplified in size and importance if they are permitted free growth, so it is best to learn the art of forgetfulness about things that are not very important in the first place.

# Moving on for the Firm

The young cartoon wife says to her husband "You'd better start looking around for somebody new, dear. My company is transferring me out of town." This jest reflects a new social phenomenon with which many families are becoming acquainted.

Not long ago the career-minded company man took for granted he would be transferred from city to city on his way up the corporate ladder. When the boss said to move, his wife packed up the household, and the kids started school in the new city. If she had reservations, she kept them to herself.

Nowadays, however, an increasing number of these wives have careers of their own, careers that contribute as importantly to family well-being as do the husbands'. Understandably, they are likely to resist the move. Or, in an increasing number of cases, it is the wife who is transferred, and the husband who balks.

Corporations go to great lengths in the development of those employees with long-range talent capabilities. Recently I became aware of such an example, when a daughter of a friend was urged by her employer to go to the Harvard Business School to get an MBA degree. The company reassigned her husband to its Boston office while his wife completed her two years at Harvard.

After she received her degree, the two were returned to the home headquarters without loss of seniority. The entire two-year experience for both of them was at the expense of the employer.

Wise corporations have recognized this problem and are now making an attempt to find new, compatible employment for the displaced spouse. This in turn has given rise to a whole new service industry: the relocation agency. A typical agency, of which there are scores scattered throughout the nation, offers information on career opportunities and job trends in the new town in the displaced spouse's field.

In addition to practical help in job hunting, relocation agencies offer assistance to the corporation in making the transferred family view the move as a positive one for all concerned. They provide clues for house-hunters, tips on moving, information on schools and other neighborhood facilities, and even pep talks for reluctant family members.

This is splendid, but it does not go far enough. Sensitive companies must not only assist in making a smooth transition, but they must also avoid penalizing an employee who chooses not to make the move. The more sophisticated corporations are going to great lengths to assist displaced spouses in finding comfortable and appropriate employment opportunities that help establish a tranquil move.

Diplomacy is a valued asset, for the happiness of the spouse, male or female, needs to be a vital consideration so that a family move benefits both parties.

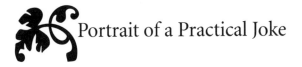

Portrait of a Practical Joke

In my younger days I was prone to play practical jokes on my good friends, but one Christmas my friends turned the tables and played a great one on me.

I had purchased a life-size oil painting of a nude female figure, painted by a young American painter named Saul Schary, and had hung it at the head of our stair landing. The subject was painted from a rear view.

Several years later, on Christmas Eve, my wife and I had stayed up until about 3:00 in the morning setting up our son's electric train and assembling our daughter's doll house. Needless to say, we were imbibing a little Christmas cheer as we worked. When all of the gifts were properly put together and placed under the Christmas tree, I started up the stairs, passed the painting, and only after I was in the bedroom did I realize that something was unusual.

I could not identify just what it was, so I retraced my steps to the ground floor. I started back up, slowly this time, and looked at the pictures lining the wall of the stairwell. When I reached the landing, I looked at the nude, and there she was in her usual location, but she had turned around, with her front view facing! This startling reversal was the cause of a sense of bewilderment, for I had seen only her back side as I traversed the stairs.

Obviously, I was flabbergasted, for never in my life had I experienced a painting turning around. I did not think I'd had too much to drink, but this phenomenon suggested that perhaps I had imbibed more than I realized. I was obviously befuzzled and confused, so my wife took pity on me and told me the story.

The front view of the original picture, in exactly the same pose and size, painted by the same artist, had been commissioned by several business associates as a surprise Christmas present, on the condition that my wife replace the original canvas with the reverse view. My bewilderment was complete. This was a genuine case of a "moving picture" show.

This experience was probably the only successful surprise that had ever been pulled on me. Surprise birthday parties had nearly always been spoiled by a careless but unintentional leak from one of the participants, but this gift, and its installation, had been guarded very carefully by the donors and by my wife.

Surprise gifts are well worth the trouble entailed. There is nothing more flattering than a present that requires time, forethought and intricate planning to execute. They reward the sender, as well as the recipient.

After having had the experience of seeing a painting turn around, I became convinced completely that I would nevermore take anything or anybody for granted.

Job Hoppers Undercut Productivity

Big business is sending its employees mixed signals, and until the confusion is straightened out, our productivity may become worse.

It has happened to all of us, or somebody we know. An employee wants a raise and a promotion, but the boss says *no*. So he finds another job with the salary and title he wants. Meanwhile, the old boss replaces the employee with somebody else, who gets the salary and position the old employee was refused.

This practice seems to be so widespread that young business school graduates are advised that the quickest way to the top is moving around to a half-dozen different jobs in five years. But such job hopping, while it may become profitable for the individual who successfully plays the game, is seriously undermining productivity.

True, the MBA accumulates a lot of experience in a half-dozen different specialties, but he develops expertise in none of them. He learns a little about many things, but not a lot about any. Certain jobs take longer to master than others, but more and more employees are job hopping so fast that the number of experts is actually decreasing.

Not only must the company lose time and money in retraining a new person for the job, but it must also pay salaries inflated by the job hoppers. But there is another reason for the job hopping that is the direct result of shortsighted top management. More and more we see examples of management tossing out its old team and bringing in a new one when profitability is lower than the board of directors wants. Instead of accepting the fact that circumstances beyond their control are at work—a recession, high interest rates or the like—the old employees get the blame, and a vicious cycle continues.

A competent hotel reservation manager is not made overnight, nor is a diamond buyer, an automobile service manager, an executive chef, an airplane pilot or a ship's captain. Only time and experience, with exposure to myriad of human problems, become the abrasive agents that hone the capacities of neophytes and make professionals out of them. Much of the public complaint about the quality of service in industry stems from the fact that there are too few experts around who know what to do and how to do it.

In my book *Quest for the Best*, I presumptuously established a list of business laws, the first of which was: "When business is good, no employee is as good as he thinks he is; when business is bad, no employee is as bad as management thinks he is."

1994

The Value of Thinking Long Term

Early in my retail career, after graduating from college, I was a floor manager in women's apparel. Several days after I started work, I had an experience which taught me a lesson of such value that it had a lasting impact on me.

A customer came to the department one morning with a box under her arm and asked for the manager. I introduced myself, and she said, "I bought this dress to wear to an important ball last Saturday night. I paid more for it than I've ever paid for a lace dress, and after one wearing, it's fallen into holes."

I examined it and made the mistake of trying to joke with her. I said, "It looks to me that you must have been wrestling in it instead of dancing." She did not think that was very funny and furiously demanded her money back. I proceeded to tell her that we could not meet her demands, on the grounds that the manufacturer would not take any responsibility for a garment that had been so badly abused.

She appealed her case to a higher court and asked me to discuss the matter with my boss. I took the dress to my father and explained that the customer had obviously damaged it, and that the manufacturer certainly would not replace it.

He looked at it and said, "Well, in the first place, what the manufacturer will do is of no consequence to the customer. She didn't buy it from him. She bought it from us. It is our responsibility and not that of the maker. In buying an expensive dress, she thought she was going to get one that would give long wear. Actually the thinner the lace, the more susceptible it is to strains."

241

He then asked, "Do you know what it costs to get a new customer?" I told him I did not, and he said, "Well, I figure it costs us about $200 to develop a customer who spends as much money a year as she does. This dress cost us $175. You are prepared to turn her down, in which case she'll never come back, and then you're going to have to go out and spend $200 to get another customer to replace her. Does that make sense?" I had to concede that it did not. "In that case," he said, "why don't you tell her we'll replace the dress, but when you do so, do it with a smile?"

I had always respected my father's ability to look ahead, but I never realized that he was omniscient. Five years later, when the great East Texas oil field blew in, this customer's husband turned out to own five square miles in the direct center of production. As a result of having satisfied her, she and her family spent several million dollars with the company in the ensuing twenty years.

Customers may not always be right, but it pays to keep them satisfied.

# A Dangerous Moralist

The person who appoints himself censor of our private lives is often one who has a guilty secret himself. This was certainly the case of Anthony Comstock, a perfectly awful man who delighted in destroying others.

Living in the late nineteenth century and first decade of the twentieth, Anthony Comstock, the guilt-ridden son of a severe, devil-fearing mother, was our country's father of censorship. Obsessed with his own sense of sin, he set about trying to make the country temptation-proof for everybody else. He vigorously lobbied congress for anti-smut laws during the Ulysses S. Grant presidency.

He was rewarded with the Comstock Act, which banned obscene materials from the mails. There were two unfortunate aspects to the bill. First, it failed to define obscenity, a problem that still plagues the courts. Second, it named Mr. Comstock himself as the post office special agent to enforce the law.

Without specific guidelines, Mr. Comstock ran amok, expanding his power to hound respectable artists, authors, newspapers and women's rights advocates, as well as pornographers and prostitutes. In the name of the law, he perpetrated outrageous injustices. He convinced a jury to convict the author of an innocuous marriage manual simply on his say-so. The book was so obscene, he explained, that he could not let the jury see it. The author killed herself.

Mr. Comstock prided himself in the fact that he drove fifteen of his victims to commit suicide rather than face public scandal.

From our more enlightened viewpoint, we can see that his obsession with sex was psychopathic. Under the guise of collecting evidence against prostitutes, for example, he once hired three women to pose naked before him—for an hour and fifteen minutes! Mr. Comstock's influence was so great that his opponents usually kept silent rather than risk his vengeance.

Anyone with a modicum of good taste deplores pornography, but the lesson of Anthony Comstock reminds us that trying to remedy the problem through censorship is like expecting the fox to guard the henhouse.

 Think Like a Customer

In an effort to attract public approval, retail stores, hotels, taxi companies and restaurants use their advertising to boast of the superior quality of their services.

They know that "good" service is a successful word to attract customers. No advertiser ever admits to "bad service" or "poor quality." To the contrary, they use and overuse "good" and "best."

Only too often the quality of service is restricted to the advertisements, and is invisible on the selling floor and on the telephone.

In a free economy, in which customers are free to exercise a choice in their purchases, superior service provides the competitive advantage that is needed when qualities are comparable.

Managements know that statement is true; they believe in it to the extent that they spend money on advertising, but frequently fail to set service standards, compensation incentives and the supervising systems to assure adequate delivery. So, as in the old German folk tale, for want of a nail, the shoe is lost; for want of a shoe, the horse is lost; for want of a horse, the rider is lost.

In consulting with clients on the techniques needed to achieve superior service, I urge them to first learn to think like a customer. It is impossible to create a service-oriented business unless the boss learns that fundamental lesson.

Once he does, everything has a tendency to fall into place, and customers rush to join the chorus of praise for a farsighted management.

Little things often give us the signs of good management. For example, taxi cab companies that have good dispatchers and who make an effort to understand the caller, stores that carry your packages to your car, restaurants that put the customer copy of the credit charge on top and the management copy beneath it (instead of vice-versa), the auto service department that attaches a brief questionnaire to your steering wheel to determine if everything was taken care of properly, the anesthesiologist who calls you a few days before an operation to reassure you that he has studied your case in advance.

These are not tricks, but are devices that prove the management's determination not only to think like a customer, but to act like one also. The most important indicator is that they care about you. All of us appreciate care.

A Dark Ages Industry

After building a new home in 1938, I concluded that the building industry was the most inefficient trade in American business. Fifty-six years later, with that previous experience having been dulled by the passage of time, the renovation of a forty-year-old house has just been completed, and my experience with it was almost exactly the same as the first time; there was no indication of the slightest improvement in the efficiency of the construction process.

From conversation with friends who have completed renovations or are in the process of doing so, I find that their horror stories of building inefficiencies, sloppy workmanship and time delays are little different from ours.

This essay is not intended to be an indictment of all the craftsmen in the building trades, the contractors who employ them, or the manufacturer suppliers of the component parts. It is rather a criticism of the process that results in economic waste, and in turn higher costs, both of which lead to disgruntlement of everybody involved.

First of all, it must be recognized that the renovation of a house, or the construction of one, is a custom job for the owners, who, in most cases, have little previous experience in the commissioning of a building. Most of them start off with a vague idea of what they want, and with an inadequate list of written definitions of their requirements. No one has schooled them in the preparatory work they must bring to their architect, such as the number and sizes of drawers, shelves, and running feet of rod space.

They know that they want power sources, but they have no idea just where they want them located, or at what height from the floor. They do not even know what a nine-foot ceiling looks like, or how high the stair risers should be.

All of these details, amplified 200 times, are what their poor architect has to wheedle from them and eventually lead them to the point of decision. There must be some who insist that their clients fill out lengthy questionnaires that cover essential information that allows them to function more efficiently. In fifty-six years, the medical profession has learned that basic written information saves both doctors and patients a lot of time.

Apparently there is erratic quality control in the factories that make lighting fixtures, appliances, metal building components, filtered glass, bathroom fixtures or hardware. It is not unusual for enameled steel framing to be painted in assorted shades of white, nor is it routine for a maker of bathroom or lighting fixtures to ship the entire order simultaneously.

A friend told me that the maker of washing machines, to whom he had complained about the thinness of the metal, advised that his criticism would be duly noted and placed in the computer. That is certainly an indication of industrial contempt for the buyer.

Housing construction is a highly competitive business, and in the efforts to supply an attractive low bid, the subcontractors frequently hire bottom-of-the-pay-scale immigrants without supplying job supervisors who speak their language or provide instructions that they can understand. No wonder they paint a wall the wrong color or misfit bathroom pipes.

A trade that works on an intermittent basis due to weather conditions loses the skills acquired in a daily job under a foreman who requires basic quality accomplishments.

The only basic charge I would make against most construction workers is that they tend to be sloppy and messy, leaving a pile of debris behind them, with little sense of job pride. As a whole, they show little respect for the work of their colleagues in the other crafts. An electrician thinks nothing of marring a carefully painted floor, and most painters do not regard paint splatter on a window or a molding as their concern.

If there have been research studies made by any of the business schools on the lack of technological and job management progress in the $122 billion home construction industry, I have been unable to locate them. Perhaps they exist, but if there have not been recent updates, this void needs to be filled. It occupies too important a part of American business, and it affects the welfare of too many craftsmen to be ignored.

Middle-class Terrorism

We deplore political terrorism, whether it comes from the radical right or the radical left. We ban the immigration of suspected professional terrorists, yet we tolerate in relative silence a greater danger to most of us—the terrorism of the radical middle class.

One of the most frightening things about political terrorism is its randomness. No matter how ordinary our daily lives, any one of us might be unlucky enough to get caught in a bombed building or a hijacked plane, or even shot at random by a passing motorist. Radical middle class terrorism also invades, with daily regularity, the lives of those in the comfortable middle class. Pick up any newspaper of any city in the United States, and you will read with shame and horror the death count of the previous twenty-four hours.

The radical middle class terrorist is the frustrated businessman who batters his wife, the mother who abuses her children in the name of discipline, the high school gangster who uses a revolver with a casualness formerly reserved for a piece of chewing gum.

To protect those dear to him, the radical middle class terrorist owns a shotgun, then uses it against his teen-age son or next-door neighbor during a petty dispute over a dented fender or a barking dog; the favorite weapon of the radical middle-class terrorist is the automobile, a projectile he uses effectively to destroy life, particularly after he has had a few drinks and is just mad at the world.

Or, if this radical fancies that he has been slurred or mistreated, his impulse is to reach for his semiautomatic weapon and spray his environment with deadly bullets.

The radical middle class terrorist is every one of us who sees or suspects such situations are developing, yet does nothing, because we think such things do not happen to nice people like us.

Violence is not solely a product of crime, poverty or political unrest. It is a problem of the radical middle class that suffers from frustrations and decides to vent them by violent action. We talk about solutions in high and low government offices, but too often our only solution approach is the wringing of hands.

We must deal seriously with our most pressing problem with a seriousness of purpose.

 A Reason To Live

There is an old Chinese folk tale about a starving beggar on the streets of Beijing who was observed with interest by a learned scholar. He watched him solicit coins from a passerby, who responded by placing two coins in the beggar's cup.

Very promptly the beggar traded his coins for a bowl of rice and a single flower. The scholar was puzzled and asked the beggar for an explanation. "I don't understand your choice; you are obviously starving, and yet you bought only one bowl of rice, spending the other coin to purchase a flower. I don't understand."

The beggar replied, "You're right; the bowl of rice will prolong my life, but the flower gives me a reason to live."

In these days of decreasing property values and increasing citizen demands for services, city leaders are hard put to balance budgets and maintain fiscal integrity. Rival civic groups have conflicting priorities. Even the omniscient King Solomon might have difficulty in making judgments that would satisfy all of the diverse demands.

One group wants potholes repaired; another seeks money to fund a neighborhood art project; others want to direct allocations from large institutions to small ones. A good case can be made for nearly all of the supplicants. Perhaps they need a dozen Solomons, or maybe one Bernard Baruch, to help solve the quandaries faced by city fathers daily.

In their deliberations, though, they might choose to recall this story of the starving beggar and recognize that life is sustained not only by the availability of food and shelter, but by the presence of beauty that creates the incentive to live.

The quality of life that makes the pursuit of existence worth the effort often lies in the abstractions caused by things of beauty—things like flowers, the sound of music, the fantasy of theater, harmonious surroundings. These are some of the qualities that make life a joy.

Even during the communist regime in Russia, gardens were maintained and manicured, the Bolshoi Ballet was vigorously supported, streets were maintained in good repair. Not so today, as the Russians seek to transform their economic system to Western-style free enterprise. The gardens of the summer palace of Peter the Great are ragged; the streets are as rough as those in some areas of Dallas; people are theoretically free, but many lack a flower to give them a reason to live.

Is Trash Telling Us Something?

During the past recession, many people developed a life-style built on the old Depression rules: *Use it up! Wear it out! Make it do! Do without!* Not everyone though, has seen fit to follow that direction. Instead they have gone in the opposite direction.

It has become an acceptable pastime of the middle class to rummage through our neighbors' cast-offs, according to a *Newsweek* item I read not long ago. The ultimate sign of hitting the economic bottom—scavenging through the dumpsters for everything from TV sets to TV dinners—seems to have gained social respectability.

Now, while I do not recommend adopting that as a hobby, I am rather pleased that some people do, since I hate to see useful things go to waste.

What puzzles me are the people who are throwing away these perfectly usable, durable goods—things like radios, lamps, furniture and appliances.

According to the scavengers, people throw away not only repairable items, but things that might need only a fresh battery or a coat of paint to work as well as ever.

Why do these things go into the garbage can, destined for oblivion in a landfill, instead of being passed on to someone who can use them?

It can't be laziness, because organizations such as the Salvation Army are only too happy to pick them up at your door. It can't be indifference either, since we are acutely aware of our precarious economic situation and our earth's finite resources.

No, our junking of so many usable items, without so much as attempting a garage sale, has a deliberate, premeditated feel to it—perhaps a feel of anger. Almost half a century of prosperity has made us a nation of consumers, yet peace of mind continues to elude us.

Could it be we are throwing away these reminders of our failure like we throw away our old flame's photograph?

Sometimes earlier civilizations tossed out their old idols when hard times or new enlightenment came along. Perhaps our bulging dumpsters mean that our long worship of materialism is nearing an end.

Label Can Be Impossible To Shake

Actors fear being typecast, because a label, once attached, is almost impossible to remove.

While I was chief executive officer of Neiman Marcus, *Women's Wear Daily*, the retail trade journal, labeled me the "melancholy Plato of retailing." The tag was bestowed on me, for I frequently was critical of fashion trends and unprogressive marketing policies. I had to smile at the dramatic ring of the phrase, although I had to admit to wearing a beard and smoking a pipe, which may have had Platonic implications. My amusement began to wear thin, however, when the term was repeated every time my name or the store's name appeared in that particular publication. I decided to do something about removing the "melancholy" label, so I went directly to the source.

A phone call to a *Women's Wear* bureau chief went like this: "To prove to your newspaper that I am not a melancholy Plato, I am going to tell you a joke."

I told her about the handbag salesman who arrived at a store's buying office for his appointment with Mrs. Jones, a tyrannical and antagonistic store buyer. Nothing ever suited her; she had to change every handle. If the bag was made in suede, she switched it to pigskin, and vice versa. But she was capable of writing such large orders that she was tolerated, although never respected by the trade or the long-suffering salesmen who were forced to deal with her.

"Mrs. Jones is not here," the receptionist told the salesman. "She passed away yesterday." The salesman looked surprised but acknowledged the information and departed. The salesman returned later that afternoon and asked again for Mrs. Jones. "I'm sorry," repeated the receptionist, but Mrs. Jones died. Didn't you understand me?" Once again, the salesman left, only to return an hour later and once more asked for Mrs. Jones. "Look," said the receptionist, "you must be some kind of nut. I've told you twice that Mrs. Jones is dead! Don't you understand me?"

"Yes, I understand you," said the salesman, "but I just love to hear you say it!"

The newspaper printed my joke, but I still was stuck with the label. Readers said it was just the kind of humor they would expect from a melancholy Plato.

When Offspring Join the Business

As a business consultant, I frequently have been confronted by problems more of a personal nature than related to business.

Businesses, of course, never can be divorced from the people who operate them, for personal problems often have an effect on efficiency. It is not uncommon to find that marital differences seriously color a corporate executive's attitudes toward his associates. In all probability, a man who is unhappy at home will be unhappy at work, and so will the people who are in his employ.

Moreover, a father-son or father-daughter relationship in a business can be difficult for both parent and child, unless the parent is extremely skillful in how he inducts his offspring into the business. It has been my observation that most children going into a family business are eager to have some degree of defined responsibility, however small, by which they can be graded. Too frequently, a parent makes the mistake of bringing a child into the business with vague duties, or even broad responsibilities that are beyond the child's capacity.

A parent can create a job for his child, but he cannot create respect from the co-workers. That accolade is one the child has to earn. I have found that more parents err in this procedure than in any other aspect of their business judgment. Often, they force the child to go into a family business for which the child has no basic interest. Then they fail to establish conditions under which the child can earn the respect of his co-workers by his own accomplishments.

258

Arbitration between parents and children is not easy. But when a reconciliation of both parties is accomplished, it is most rewarding. Good solutions mean that the egos of parent and child are protected and that both learn for the first time what goals the other is seeking. There can be no victories, only understanding.

Everyone in life is entitled to a shot at happiness, and no parent has the right to force his child into the parent's occupation. The child is entitled to decide for himself what he wants to do, even if the wrong choice is made. Very seldom are career selections irrevocable, and changes of mind must be accepted as indications of intellectual and emotional growth, never with words of retribution. Every time I help in that process, I feel like a healer.

Leadership and Good Taste

The magazine *Advertising Age* published an article asking its readers in the advertising profession what were the qualities that made a bad client.

One of the answers to its query came from an old-timer in the agency business who said, "It's hard to pick one worst characteristic from the examples you mention. Most really bad clients have them all. If it all comes down to one common denominator, though, I'd have to say it is bad taste. To me the worst client is guilty of the worst taste. The best clients are to be admired for their good taste. This reply stimulated me to ask a buyer in a department store, 'What percentage of bad taste merchandise do you buy?' She replied, 'About forty percent. If I don't, I'd miss a lot of sales.'"

I don't agree with the department store buyer, for I believe that such a philosophy succeeds in creating a forty percent bad taste standard for the store. An uneducated market will take time to become savvy, but the rate of education is determined by the skill and determination of the retailers and by the existence of a sophisticated peer group. The latter can be a potent educational influence.

Some years ago, I wrote a piece for the *Atlantic Monthly* entitled "Fashion Is My Business," in which I discussed this subject. I wrote, "The taste of the general public isn't as good as that of the sophisticated minority, but it isn't as irrevocably bad as many manufacturers and retailers believe it may be. The public will buy bad taste merchandise if it has no choice, but it will usually respond affirmatively to any product in good taste if it is presented at the right time with authority."

If there is no resistance to bad taste in advertising, automobile manufacturing, home decorating, clothes, landscaping, building architecture, and product design in general, then the whole culture will shift to the lowest level. There is historical evidence of nations whose national tastes range from indifferent to mediocre, while others like France and Italy have earned worldwide reputations for being the standard bearers of good taste.

The store buyer was guilty of taking the line of the least resistance by creating a false identity for her company. She is creating a sense of customer confusion as to what her store actually stands for. The store that panders to the lowest level of taste will eventually find itself outstripped by competitors who believe just the opposite. Stores and advertising agents have a responsibility to lead public taste—not yield to it.